WALKING IN THE
LIGHT

WALKING IN THE
LIGHT

Knowing and Doing God's Will

STEVE HARPER

UPPER
ROOM BOOKS®
NASHVILLE

Cover image:
Cover design: Bruce Gore / gorestudio.com

LIBRARY OF CONGRESS CATALOGING-IN-PUBLICATION DATA
Harper, Steve, 1947–
  Walk in the light : knowing and doing God's will / Steve Harper.
    pages cm
  ISBN 978-0-8358-1344-0 (print) —ISBN 978-0-8358-1345-7 (mobi) —
ISBN 978-0-8358-1346-4 (epub)
1. Christian life. 2. Spirituality—Christianity. 3. Spiritual
life—Christianity. 4. Walking—Religious aspects—Christianity.
5. Light—Religious aspects—Christianity. I. Title.
  BV4501.3.H366 2014
  248.4—dc23
                                                          2013049097

Printed in the United States of America

CONTENTS

INTRODUCTION

We pray to know God's will because we believe it can be known. We do not believe that God is playing cat-and-mouse with us, much less trying to avoid us or keep us in the dark. On the contrary, we believe God to be a God of revelation. Certainly, God's thoughts are not our thoughts, and God's ways *are* higher than our ways (Isa. 55:8-9). We will never fully or perfectly discern God's will on every occasion. We will always pray to know God's will in the context of mystery. But because we are made in the image of God, we have a created instinct to "walk and talk" with God—to hear God's voice and to obey God's will. We come with a built-in desire for discernment!

But even as we acknowledge our hunger to know and to do God's will, we find ourselves struggling to do so—not only because of our sinfulness (as we prefer our will to God's will) but because of our lack of certainty that an idea or impression actually reflects God's will. We experience moments of inspiration, but often an accompanying confusion leaves us hesitant to put them into action. Consequently, we feel a tension between our desire to know God's will and our confidence in doing it.

This tension can result in a spiritual paralysis that keeps us from doing what we have been impressed to do, which further confuses us and leaves us wondering if our failure to act was (or was not) God's will.

But this confusion and tension is not God's wish for us. Discernment, while an inexact experience, is not supposed to be a fearful one. God does not want our hesitancy to deteriorate into passivity or inaction. Instead, God has provided insights from scripture and tradition to help us cultivate our praying to know God's will. In this book I will share some of my insights and invite you on a journey that can enhance your joy in finding and following God's will.

We will approach our subject first by looking at principles that have undergirded Christian discernment over the centuries—a foundation to lay prior to any act of praying to know God's will. And then, we will build on that foundation by exploring selected practices that can facilitate our discovery and enactment of God's will. The primary image we will use is that of walking. Each chapter will describe steps to take in relation to the subject at hand. These steps, when taken, can create a journey. But even the longest journey is nothing more than a combination of small steps. In each chapter we will examine some little steps that can take us farther into praying to know God's will. We will capture these like snapshots in an album, so that we can continue to ponder them and be encouraged by what we see.

We do all this as Christians in community, not as isolated believers. Discernment has never been viewed as something a person does alone. We often have to make decisions and take actions on our own, but even then we do not do this apart from insights and encouragement we receive from others, both ancient and modern. As your brother in Christ, I will write as honestly as I can about this subject; I will not treat it casually or superficially. Praying to know God's will must not fall prey to clichés. Rather, it must become part and parcel of our ongoing life of prayer. I pray that what you are about to read will help it become so for you. Blessings!

—STEVE HARPER

WALKING IN THE LIGHT

My dad was a walker. As a child, I recall his deciding to walk to work rather than drive. He would set off on his journey of a little over a mile with a spring in his step, usually whistling as he headed into town. Even now I can close my eyes and see him walking along. It seemed to me as if he could walk forever; I remember trying to keep up with him, whether on the sidewalk or on the golf course. Until his death, Dad enjoyed walking. I think walking made him feel alive.

Maybe those memories of my dad have made me stop and pay attention to the notion of walking when it comes up in the Bible. In the opening chapters of scripture, we discover God walking in the garden (Gen. 3:8). Not long after, the Bible states that Enoch "walked with God" (Gen. 5:22). And as the biblical picture unfolds, we see individuals and groups walking. "The Christian walk" has become a metaphor for describing our relationship with God. It is a good one to help us find and do God's will.

John the elder wrote to some friends and told them to "walk in the light" (1 John 1:7). His advice did not specifically relate to discerning God's will, but he was commending a way of relating to God—who is light (1 John 1:5). By using this phrase in our exploration of discernment we are reminded that discernment is not a technique. It is a disposition of our heart to discover and then do the will of God. The image of "walking in the light" becomes a rich one that makes praying to know God's will dynamic and inviting. And it connects discernment to the larger spiritual journey.

Our first step involves embracing the truth that God is Light. We begin our walk with the conviction that God is a God of revelation. Light shines; it does not keep to itself. It shines to manifest itself and to dispel darkness. Similarly, God's nature is to reveal. But at the same time, we must not view discernment as a process that will give us perfect understandings or explanations. Praying to know God's will does not eliminate mystery. It does not promote an ironclad guarantee of absolute correctness. It simply means that we approach the discernment process with humility. God's will is not a complete unknown.

In many aspects of our lives we operate with less than complete knowledge. Every time I turn on an electronic device, I enter a world that I do not understand. When I stop to think about it, that is the case in many aspects of my life. But a partial understanding of things is enough to keep moving forward. I believe God's will operates the same way. God enables us to know enough to make progress. We move into discernment in a step-by-step fashion. Our willingness to walk in the light that we have received implies our trust of a God who will give us more light

The second step embraces our trusting that there is no darkness at all in God. I believe the will of God is always good.[1] Life itself is not always good, because we live in a fallen world. But we must never equate our circumstances with God's nature. Despite Adam and Eve's decision and the resulting fallenness of our world, God's nature remains one of love.[2] The work of God since the Fall has been that of redemption—leading us away from temptation and delivering us from evil. We see this in the imagery of light because it illumines our path and enables us to walk past obstacles. With light we can find passageways through fences and ladders to climb over walls. And even when we are stymied, light allows us to see places for rest before resuming the journey. So we pray to know God's will in order to find and follow the way of divine goodness, the way that God has in mind for us.

Our third step comes in realizing that we never experience all the light at once. Light shines beyond where we walk. As the day progresses, more light comes from the sun to us. At no time do we get *all* the light. So too, God's will is never "total" in a given moment. In fact, the Greek word that John uses in his letter is in the present tense, connoting ongoing action. We walk in the light . . . and keep walking. Discernment as an ongoing process means the journey never ends. Our present enlightenment illumines the path enough to take the next step. We never see fully or all the way to the end. Praying to know God's will is a step-by-step, little-by-little experience. It is an experience in which God is the giver, and we are the receivers. Praying to know God's will requires listening, putting ourselves into the position of receptivity, and then taking the next few steps in relation to what we have seen and heard.

Our fourth step entails walking as the pattern of our life. God leads; we follow. Our faith journey begins that way and continues in that fashion to the end. Recognizing this, we increasingly establish the rhythm of listening and responding, which is the essence and sequence of prayer. Jesus modeled this pattern in his own life and ministry by regularly withdrawing from people and ministry to pray (Luke 5:15-16). He invited the apostles to do the same (Mark 6:31). His action and invitation implies that discernment is not an occasional act but rather a disposition of heart and will. We say with the psalmist, "I delight to do your will, O my God" (Psalm 40:8).

A fifth step engages our will so that walking is a participatory action. We have to be in motion in order to walk. We do not go for a hike by reading a book about hiking. Even when we read about the benefits of walking, we must actually walk in order to receive them. In terms of the spiritual life, our acting on what we know is even more important. God is on the move. God's will is not locked in the past or static in the present—it is unfolding. God calls us to "walk in the light" as those who actively participate in knowing and doing God's will. We express this reality every time we pray the Lord's Prayer: "Thy kingdom come. Thy will be done in earth, as *it is* in heaven" (Matt. 6:10, KJV). As we pray this prayer, day after day, we commit ourselves to being cocreators with God.

Years ago, I discovered that Frank Laubach prayed the following prayer at the beginning of every day: "God, what are you doing in the world today that I can help you with?"[3] I have made Laubach's question a mainstay in my morning prayer. It expresses a question of discernment that seeks to know and do the will of God. It is a prayer of faith—a prayer that believes in God's active involvement in every area of life. And it is a prayer that tells me I am invited to participate in some (not all) of what God is doing. I have found that simply praying this prayer ignites a spirit of adventure, summoning me to an experience with my heavenly Father, similar to the experience I had with my dad when he would decide to go for a walk and say to me, "Come on along." That's what I hear God saying as we begin this book, and the good news is that we do it "walking in the light."

Questions for Reflection and Discussion

- What comes to your mind when you connect discernment with the image of walking?
- Which of the five "steps" spoke to you the most? Why?
- In what area of your life do you feel God is asking for your help?

Chapter 2

GETTING OFF TO A GOOD START

I remember when and where each of our children began to walk. Jeannie, my wife, and I have pictures that capture the experience; but even if we didn't, the memories remain very much alive in our minds and hearts. We knew the time was approaching; we encouraged them to pull up, stand on their feet, and give it a try. But the moment when they took a step on their own, their "first," was a moment filled with surprise and excitement. It was a big deal, and we wanted John and Katrina to know how proud we were of them. We clapped and shouted. We hugged them and ruffled their hair. We celebrated!

Then Jeannie and I began to help our children. We supported and instructed them. We pointed out the safe places to walk. We showed them how to hold on to handrails when they needed additional support. We wanted them to get off to a good start, because we knew they had commenced a never-ending journey. Their first steps would be followed by millions and billions more. They were on their way to places they could not imagine, and their walking would bring them into experiences they could not predict. They were walking!

Praying to know God's will resembles that experience. Our commitment to "walk in the light" gives us a wonderful moment of joy that contains the seeds of something more. So we celebrate the launch but acknowledge the importance of getting off to a good start. Our instinctive desire to find and follow God's will does not mean we automatically know how to do it well. Just because we are made to walk does not mean we will always head in the right direction. And unfortunately, as I have sought to discern the will of God myself and to help others do so, I have found a fair amount of misinformation and misconception floating around. We must not attach false notions to our journey. Otherwise, we will be hindered, deceived, and prevented from walking in the light as God intends. To ignore them will almost certainly draw us off the path. Let's look at several of these misconceptions.

The first misconception comes in believing that discernment is a quality that we possess We can falsely presume that if we have "it," that our job is now to force "it" upon everyone else. We begin to act with an attitude that says, "I know God's will, but you don't." Individuals can wreak havoc on congregations with this idea. And churches get into difficulty when they come to believe that their way of looking at a situation is the *only* way to view it: "We have the one and only truth on this matter, which means if you don't see it our way, you are wrong!" Stories of people who have used the will of God as a weapon—not only against the bad, old sinful world but also against other Christians—fill the pages of history. Even praying to know the will of God can end up as a spiritual version of a soft-drink taste test with one group believing its beverage is superior to the other.

Praying rightly to know the will of God requires a differentiation between doctrine and opinion. Doctrines, or fundamental beliefs, can be held by Christians across the board. Opinions are the particular interpretations of those beliefs that may be held by one group but not another. In praying to know God's will, we pray to discover the doctrines, leaving the opinions (application of beliefs) to the inevitable variations in time, place, and circumstance. When we pray to know God's will, we pray that the Spirit will place us in fellowship with the rest of the body of Christ. True discernment always strengthens community, even if it challenges community occasionally.

For example, I might pray to know God's will in relation to the Bible. When I do so, I will find that the holy scriptures are to be the inspired and primary means of grace in my life and in the life of the Christian community. That is a belief. But when I go on to pray concerning how I am to make the Bible central in my spiritual formation, I find that the plan I follow may differ from that of another disciple. I may be learning to pray the psalms, while another Christian is finding out more of who Jesus is by reading systematically through the Gospels.

Both believers have come to know God's will correctly. One is no more correct than the other. Both live out a doctrine (universal conviction) of the Bible's significant and normative influence on a Christ follower's life. But that does not occur in only one way.

We embrace **a second misconception** when we think that we must get it right the first time around or all the time. This misconception will lead us into the fear of failure. Instead, we realize that God allows for trial-and-error in the midst of devotion. Faithfulness, not success, marks the discerning heart. God commends our desire to do God's will, as we saw previously in Psalm 40:8. With that desire comes God's permission to fail. Not acknowledging God's permission-giving makes discernment a fear-based process rooted in perfectionism, rather than a faith-based endeavor rooted in sacred trial-and-error. To fall into this trap is to turn a dynamic process into a passive one—a process that disengages our spirit from the Holy Spirit. We will never discover how to practice discernment unless we are willing to include failure (and learning from it) as part of the experience.

I tell people that they can always make a U-turn on God's highway. To state it theologically, the same Spirit that invites us to live for the glory of God will convict us when our attempt to do so is incorrect. It's called repentance. It's the work of the Spirit enabling us to "change our mind" and "alter our will" (*metanoia*) after we have headed in a particular direction. Why do we trust God's help on the front end of a decision and then believe God will abandon us as we seek to carry it out? God guides us all along the way—not simply when we set out.

Supposedly an assistant approached Thomas Edison one day and commented, "Mr. Edison, you must be deeply discouraged. You have tried so many times to make a light bulb, but each time you've failed." Edison replied, "Discouraged? By no means! I now know hundreds of ways not to make a light bulb." Edison took the accumulated knowledge of his defeats and used them to move toward his eventual victory. I would guess that Edison's experience is the way most achievements happen—that is, only after previous failures and alterations made along the way.

Praying to know God's will flows along the same lines. We set out to do God's will only to find we've set out in the wrong direction—or at least gone somewhat off course. The Holy Spirit convicts us about it and helps us make a midcourse correction. I believe Psalm 23 expresses a similar conviction when the psalmist states, "You anoint my head with oil." A sheep needs that kind of anointing only when it has wounded its head in a bramble bush or in a skirmish with another sheep. The oil is both the indicator that the sheep has made a mistake and the means to bring healing out of it. The mistakes we make in praying to know God's will can actually heal us from perfectionism and send us back into the discernment process with greater wisdom.

A third misconception occurs when we believe the will of God is a static reality. This leads us into stagnation. In praying to know God's will, one discovery leads to another. We move ahead little by little. Discernment often comes through incremental actions, not leaps and bounds. We live through spiritual "seasons"—some abundantly productive and others barren and dead. But every moment is a God moment because God is light all the time. The sun never ceases to shine; the Spirit never ceases to work in us.

I describe the fundamental stages using the words *learner, leader,* and *light.* We do not leave one stage behind and move to the next one. I affirm a recognizable progression to finding and following the will of God. We all begin as *learners.* Our basic disposition must be one of receptivity—one of submission to the collective wisdom of the church through scripture and tradition. We come to discernment with a spirit that says, "I do not know, but I want to know." And then, as we ask, seek, and knock we are given, we find, and a door is opened. At that point, we become *leaders*—men and women who now activate the will of God in concrete situations. We practice our faith. We live most of our lives in this second phase. Almost everything we say and do enacts some kind of decision.

Beyond the stages of being learners and leaders, there awaits a third stage—a time when we are expected to profess more than we produce—a time to live in the community as matriarchs and patriarchs who say by the wisdom of years, "This is true, and it works!" In this Stage, we become God's instruments to guide and encourage others. We no longer reside on the cutting edge and, truth be told, we understand that our time to be there has passed. That place goes to a new generation, just as our predecessors stepped aside so that we could lead in our day. And if we live into this third stage, we will find it to be as valuable and meaningful as the previous two. Praying to know God's will is not a static endeavor but a never-ending journey.

Many people embrace **a fourth misconception** by thinking that God's will opposes their desires. This can lead us into dualism—into treating our will and God's will as separate entities. I believe this idea comes from our failure to remember that not only is God light, God is also love. And much of the time, the will of God will be what produces our greatest joy. Holiness and happiness are siblings.

At times God leads us differently than we might prefer and offers us a challenging course of action. Sometimes doing the will of God is painful. It was so for Jesus, especially in relation to the cross, "who for the sake of the joy that was set before him endured the cross" (Heb. 12:2). His joy was not in the pain of the nails but in the fulfillment of his purpose to seek and to save the lost. His discernment of God's will reached its climax in the garden of Gethsemane when he prayed, "Not my will but yours be done." And in praying this, he reminds us that discernment and hardship sometimes go together. Across the years of my life, I have been awed to know men and women who have endured great trials for Christ and who have done so with the joy of the Lord as their strength.

A fifth misconception occurs when we think that we must know the will of God down to the last detail before making a move. This idea can lead to spiritual paralysis. Often discernment is more like following a map than being handed a specific address. A map first tells me that I am in the vicinity; then I pursue the necessary actions to nail down the specifics. In terms of the will of God, I describe the "vicinity" using the nine words we call the fruit of the Spirit: love, joy, peace, patience, kindness, gentleness, faithfulness, generosity, and self-control (Gal. 5:22-23). As Paul notes, the Spirit produces this fruit, and what the Spirit produces is never contrary to the will of God. Furthermore, I have discovered that Jesus himself demonstrated these qualities. So we are living the Christlike life when we manifest the fruit of the Spirit.

I have worked with students most of my professional life. I have witnessed their struggles in praying to know God's will regarding their education. Sometimes they get overwhelmed in trying to figure out which school to attend; they get bogged down in making a final decision. When this is the case, I have said to them, "Why don't you accept the will of God as that of your going to school and then believe that God gives you the freedom to choose the school you will attend?" Sometimes people have responded, "You mean I don't have to know the exact school?" And I have replied, "Not right now. The emphasis comes in your discerning that God wills you to get an education and then to trust that you can get one in more than one institution." Praying to know God's will often joins God's guidance to our explorations. God's impressions and our common sense often combine when finding and following God's will.

For example, we believe that God wills us to love, and we realize that in any given situation more than one way to love exists. God's will is to love; the way we love is left to our free choice. The same holds true for the other fruit of the Spirit. The fruit is the divine principle, and the Spirit entrusts the fruit's expression to human freedom. We fall within the vicinity of God's will when we live in relation to the fruit of the Spirit. And as we do that, we relax and express the fruit in details that may not always be clearly revealed and certainly not always expressed in a one-size-fits-all result.

A final misconception occurs when we equate the will of God with what *others* think we should do—or worse, expect us to do. Later we will explore the value and necessity of Christian community in the discernment process. But right now, let's understand that what others think we should do and what God thinks we should do are not always the same. I have seen Christians oppressed by mentors, guides, and leaders who said directly or in effect, "If you want to do God's will, you have to do what I say." This approach is nothing other than spiritual manipulation.

I have known children whose parents oppressed them by demanding that they go in a set direction, attend a certain school, or go into a particular line of work. The parents' attempted to have a life through their children that they did not have on their own or tried to maintain control over their children even after they became adults. This oppression is a misunderstanding of how a person finds God's will, and it can derail people from finding that will for years.

My point is that the will of God and the will of people do not always match. Happily, we do receive wise counsel from family members and friends who have lived life ahead of us. When that is the case, we receive their advice and put it into practice. But discernment involves praying to know and do God's will, and sometimes that will mean disappointing others who have fixed ideas and opinions about what we should do with our lives. Praying to know God's will is an act of courage, an act that sometimes compels us to swim upstream in order for the will of God to be born.

If we can recognize these errors and embrace their corrections, we can move into the upcoming elements of this book with confidence. We will discover that praying to know God's will is possible, purposeful, and flat-out fun. And knowing that, we can move out as adventurers, following the God who joyfully reveals the divine will.

Questions for Reflection and Discussion

- Which misconception spoke to you the most? Why?
- What stage or "season" (learner, leader, light) are you in? What does that stage reveal to you about discernment?
- What is your heart's desire right now? How do you see God's will in it?

Chapter 3

WALKING WITH AN OPEN HEART

I feel blessed to have been married to my wife, Jeannie, for almost forty-five years. One blessing comes through her positive approach to life. She sees life as an adventure. She approaches each day with an open heart, ready to embrace whatever it may hold. I have seen this openness manifest itself in times of joy and sorrow, celebration and challenge. Her capacity to do this comes, in part, from her parents and the way they taught her to live. But much of it results from her decision to view the universe as friendly. Not everyone shares her view. Over the years, I have met people who approach their lives with caution, even trepidation. The spirit and substance of their lives differ from those who walk with an open heart.

Discernment is related to our ability to walk with an open heart. We do so because we believe God is love. We have nothing to fear. We live in a friendly universe. While we will never fully comprehend this notion, God invites us into life as a sacred dance, as an adventure to anticipate, not a peril to avoid. Praying to know God's will can only exist for the long haul when we believe that God's will always favors our best interests. We ask, seek, and knock with trust, expectancy, and adventure.

One biblical image I use to express this openheartedness is "incline your hearts to the LORD." It appears first in Joshua 24:23, when the people of Israel renew their covenant with God. The renewal is not just re-signing a contract; it signals re-offering hearts to God. The image of "inclining" their hearts is both telling and inviting. Conceive of it like raising a board from where we are to where God is. This responsive act to God's grace creates a spiritual "law of gravity." Whatever God wishes to roll our way, will travel down that board (taken here to mean our prayers to know God's will) and find lodging in our hearts. The raising of our hands in worship symbolizes this receptivity. It is a physical act that says to God, "I am inclining my heart to you; whatever you want to send my way will make its home in me." So discernment is more a disposition of our hearts than a particular technique. As we begin our journey to know and do the will of God, it's important to explore some steps we take in becoming people with open hearts.

The first step is walking with a capable heart. God has created this capability in us through what the Bible calls "the image of God" (Gen. 1:26-28). This image, this "likeness," gives us the capacity for a relationship with God. Adam and Eve walked and talked with God in Eden. We can converse with God because we have been created for communion. Discernment is rooted in the reality of Spirit-to-spirit communication, heart-to-heart interaction. Some call this "attentiveness," which portrays a heart that's capable of being in touch with God.

I remember as a child hearing our church sing the gospel hymn "Turn Your Radio On." The song's lyrics suggest that the soul is a spiritual radio made to receive God's signals—but it has to be turned on. So we sang, "Get in touch with God, turn your radio on." We had annual revivals and other emphases to keep our "radios" in good shape and turned on. My church's underlying conviction was that God had created us for fellowship and interaction. The old radio image accurately describes the capable heart. Right now, hundreds of radio and television signals are passing through the places where we live. Invisible Internet data is ready to be retrieved through our computers or mobile devices. But we must turn the devices "on." Attentiveness is the soul's switch, the starting point for an open heart.

Attentiveness is not easy to come by these days. Our world moves at breakneck speed 24/7, and we are caught up in the activity. Some of this activity lies beyond our ability to choose. Tasks and messages come at us much faster than we can process them. Out of sheer survival, we have become a planet that reacts rather than responds. We don't have time to think; we only have time to act. We have to complete our tasks; otherwise the tasks pile up. This kind of living turns our radios off, and we become people who live without messages. We resemble the Japanese soldiers found on South-Pacific islands years after World War II was over. They didn't know the war was over because they had lost communication with the outside world. So they stayed at their posts, fighting a war that no longer existed!

We are living souls made in God's image, but our never-ending round of feverish activity has damaged our spiritual radios. Consequently, we do not receive the messages God sends us. Or, at best, we receive garbled messages as they come to us from the mix of life. We live on automatic pilot and hope for the best rather than take the time to stop, look, listen—and discover the will of God. We know this is so because we experience moments when we acknowledge from within that "this is not the way God intended for us to live." And as we shall see farther along in this book, walking in the light often means first coming out of the dark.

Praying to know God's will is increasingly countercultural. It rejects the "shoot first and ask questions later" mentality, refusing to "fly by the seat of our pants." We cease to be three miles wide and a half-inch deep by trading superficiality for substance. Like the tribes of Israel, we choose to renew the covenant by inclining our hearts to God. It is claiming our capable heart and allowing God to speak life-giving words into it, so that we can be responsive rather than reactive. It is walking with a capable heart.

We take **our second step** in openheartedness by walking with a confident heart. We have alluded to this confidence more than once, as we have laid down the notion that God desires that we know God's will. Trust is one of the threads that winds its way through the tapestry of discernment. We live with mystery, but we seek revelation. The space between what we can know and what we will never know is called wonder. We all have had those moments when we experienced wonder—a sight, a sound, an impression that opened the way to purpose and progress. Wonder does not eliminate mystery; it receives it as insight and inspiration for the continuing journey.

Years ago, I was involved in a discernment process about the possibility of a new ministry opportunity. I pursued the search process as a way of learning more about the position and also as a way to see whether or not I fit the profile. One morning I was reading a passage from E. Stanley Jones, and as I did so, his words became the means God used to make it immediately and perfectly clear that I should remove myself from the search process. It was a decisive moment—and simultaneously a scary one, because I had to act on the revelation I had received. I had to call the chair of the search committee and take myself out of the running.

I still recall that as one of the hardest decisions I have ever made, because I sincerely believed the new ministry was worthwhile and that I would find it meaningful if I were chosen to do it. But the message had come; I was not to continue in the process. So, I telephoned the chair and told him my decision. Due to his familiarity with E. Stanley Jones, he understood it when I said, "This morning, Brother Stanley told me I must withdraw from the search process." It's still a moment both of us remember. That moment could only have come out of trust—out of a confident heart.

I speak with people all the time who have experienced moments like this and, like me, they have acted on them. Often they will celebrate the outcome. But I honestly say that they sometimes admit that they made a mistake by acting on the impression. That's why we have already stated that discernment is not always "getting it right." A confident heart is not an arrogant heart or a never-failing heart. A confident heart simply trusts and can say with the psalmist, "He leads me" (23:2). A confident heart acts on the best available evidence, realizing that even if the decision turns out to be wrong, it is not the end of the world.

In this regard, I have come to think of discernment as a spiritual exercise—a repeated practice that strengthens our "muscle" for knowing and doing God's will. The old adage that "practice makes perfect" has relevance. We rarely do something the first time as well as we do it later. The same holds true for praying to know God's will. It may begin with a heavy dose of "hope so, think so" and then gradually grow into confidence. I have read hundreds of books written by the saints of the ages, and I have not found a single person who didn't include a certain amount of sanctified trial and error. But the ability to trust, coupled with the willingness to act, strengthens the powers of discernment that we seek. We walk with a confident heart.

Our third step is walking with a consecrated heart. This may appear obvious, but it isn't. I have found myself saying that I wanted to know the will of God but later realized that I didn't. Saint Augustine said that he used to pray "thy kingdom come; thy will be done" but then secretly put in the phrase "but not now." Several times Jesus raised the question "What do you want me to do for you?" Sometimes a person's condition made the question appear ridiculous, but Jesus knew that he or she had to be part of the process. Those with whom he raised this question had to accept and willingly put into practice what he was about to do. Similarly, praying to know the will of God rests upon the prior commitment to do God's will once we know it. And sometimes, our language of desire is not rooted in our actual intentions. A superficial piety can say the right words without having the necessary willpower to make the words real. It's the difference between attending a Bible study and engaging in Bible living.

Romans 12:1-2 directly connects the engagement of the will to knowing the will of God. We will explore these verses in greater detail later in the book; but for now, we need to understand the flow of the passage. Paul begins with the exhortation to the Roman Christians to "present your bodies . . . to God" (v. 1). The body meant more than the physical; it stood for the whole person. This is the initiating factor in what follows; namely, knowing the will of God (v. 2). The passage flows from engagement, to surrender, to discernment.

I believe that the next edition of a hymnal should include "The Hokey Pokey." This dance song begins with putting a hand in and moves along until we put our "whole self" in. At that point, everyone sings, "That's what it's all about!" The same is true with respect to praying to know God's will. We may begin with dipping a spiritual toe into the water. We may play at it halfheartedly for a while. But the end is to dive in and be submerged in the water of life. That's what it's all about!

The classical word for this diving in is *abandonment*. People use the phrase "let go and let God" to describe it. But whatever we call it, we mean that the life of faith and the discovery of God's will rests upon our willingness to surrender ourselves to God. The false self resists to the death this surrender.[4] The false self will even appear religious so long as religion doesn't get soul deep. Satan will allow us to dabble in churchianity, so long as it keeps us from embracing Christianity. But Jesus eventually comes and asks us, just like he did the folks in scripture, "What do you want me to do for you?" And when our words flow from our will, situations begin to change. When we put our "whole self" in, we more readily discover the will of God than when we only fain desire for it.

The realization of this desire sometimes has amazing consequences. It moves people to take up tasks they never imagined themselves doing. It inspires people to take risks. It enables people to face sufferings and challenges, acknowledging that God's will is not always easy and comfortable. We no longer demand that life turn out okay. Abandonment puts us in league with Christ, who "for the sake of the joy that was set before him endured the cross" (Heb. 12:2). Walking with a consecrated heart places us in God's hands, and our hearts find rest because, as Saint Augustine put it, our hearts will always be restless until they rest in God.

Think of the will of God like rain. If we run outside to capture some of the water, we go with an uncovered bucket. Rain can only fill an open bucket. Similarly, when it comes to praying to know God's will, our hearts must be open. Our radios must be on. Our souls must be receptive. Otherwise, the "rain of God" will splash off and never soak our lives. Now may be a good to time to renew your covenant with God—a time to incline your heart to the Lord and say, "God, I am willing to walk with an open heart, knowing that this is the starting point for any and all discernment." As I have written these words, I have opened my heart yet again. Everything that follows depends on it.

Questions for Reflection and Discussion

- What do words like *dance* and *adventure* tell you about discernment?
- How do busyness and superficiality affect discernment?
- In what areas of your life do you have a "covered bucket"? How does this keep you from finding and following God's will?

WALKING WITH A
FORMED HEART

As I grew up, my dad tracked my growth by having me stand against the door frame leading into my bedroom. As I strained to add as much height as I possibly could, he would take his thumbnail and press it into the wood, leaving a little notch. Those notches remained in the door frame long after I left home. They were Dad's way of measuring my development and showing me that I was growing.

In the last chapter I noted that discernment begins with an open heart. But it cannot and must not stop there. An open heart, while wonderful and necessary, can be dangerous. A bucket that is open at the top and the bottom will not hold any water. Our hearts must be formed. Discernment moves beyond praying for openness to God's leading to praying to become shaped in increasing conformity to Jesus. The Incarnation reveals what redeemed humanity looks like. In being fully human, Jesus gives us an example to follow. The Sermon on the Mount is the fundamental description that Jesus used to describe a life in alignment with God's will. We will use it to describe several key steps in another aspect of praying to know God's will: walking with a formed heart.

The first step is repentance. A while back, I realized that the Sermon on the Mount actually begins *before* Jesus sits down to deliver it in Matthew 5. It begins when Jesus calls people to repent (Matt. 4:17). We immediately notice that Jesus is proclaiming John's message (Matt. 3:2), which signals that his ministry will continue the previous covenant God had made. We step into the Christian stream, which itself flows from the long and rich stream captured for us in the Old Testament. The gospel is "good news" in part because it remains in keeping with everything God originally designed and set forth in the history of Israel. Christianity is not an aberration; it is a fulfillment. And like the message of the Hebrew Scriptures, the Christian gospel begins with the call to repentance. We must not miss this; otherwise, we will not understand discernment in the fullest possible way.

Misconceptions regarding repentance abound. Many of them are negative, even repulsive. Consequently, people shy away from it. They fight it, sometimes for years. But when we associate repentance with the life and ministry of Jesus, we recognize it as part of the gospel, part of the good news God wants to tell us—the beginning part. In its essence, repentance means to have a change of mind and heart. Jesus' call to repentance is his way of asking this question: "Are you willing to look at life in a new way?"

The old way of viewing life through the consequences of sin disposes our hearts to be self-centered, self-referencing, self-promoting, and self-reliant. When Jesus tells us to repent, he is inviting us to look at life differently. He is asking us, "Are you willing to look at life from a new angle—no longer from the angle of your own egotism but from the vantage point of God? Are you willing to view life the way it looks on God's terms rather than your own?" That's what it means to repent.

Praying to know God's will is a fundamental act of repentance. It is our way of saying to God, "I am willing to look at life from your point of view. I am willing to change my mind and heart and no longer look at life through the lens of my ego." That is where the formation of a discerning heart begins, where the gospel begins, where life (abundant and everlasting) begins. Discernment offers a powerful way to deny the lure of egotism and discover the life of God in our souls. It is simultaneously an act of defiance and an act of devotion. So, in the context of walking with a formed heart, we begin with repentance. We begin where Jesus began, and we respond to the question he asked by saying, "I am willing to change my way of looking at things. I am willing to let you show me what life looks like. I want to know your will." This is our first step in learning to walk with a formed heart.

The second step follows. Notice in Matthew's narrative that Jesus does not move immediately from repentance to the Sermon on the Mount. Instead, Matthew captures two events that define our second step of following. He writes about Jesus' calling the first apostles (4:18-22) and then about Jesus' first ministry tour out of which "great crowds followed him" (4:25). From a spiritual formation standpoint, following Jesus is the necessary consequence of being open to him. I may say I am open to someone or something but only when I exercise my will do I move my life from an alleged openness to an actual one. Walking with a formed heart means that I not only say I am willing to let Jesus show me a new way of life; I actually follow him into the discovery of that life.

This following is a lifelong process. Read the Gospels to see that the disciples not only began to follow Jesus, but they continued to follow him. Many turned away in the course of the journey; a few stayed with him. Jesus' death almost canceled the enterprise, but the Holy Spirit's work in the hours after the crucifixion kept the whole thing from falling apart. Similarly, in our journey with Jesus we face many temptations to throw in the towel; but if we remain receptive to the Spirit, we will receive fresh experiences that will renew and strengthen us. We never cease to be followers of Christ. Even after the Resurrection the disciples continued to follow and to be formed through the Spirit at work in the church in ways even their time with Jesus had not provided. Our experience will be the same.

Dr. J. C. McPheeters served as the second president of Asbury Theological Seminary. Jeannie and I were privileged and blessed to know him. In fact, he was still alive when I returned to the seminary in 1980 to serve as a professor. At ninety years of age, "Dr. Mac" preached his last sermon in Estes Chapel. Of course, he didn't know it would be his final sermon. On that final occasion, Dr. McPheeters chose this as the topic for that message: "The New Things God Is Teaching Me." I left the service in tears, walking back to my office, praying that the holy mantle that had fallen on Dr. Mac would also fall on me; that is, the mantle of living so long and so close to Jesus, that at age ninety (should I live that long) I could stand in front of a group of people and tell them the new things God is teaching me!

This is what it means to follow Jesus. We can mark the beginning point of the journey, but we can never state the ending date of it. We move increasingly into the infinity of God. How can we ever get to the end of that? We always have another step to take, another lesson to learn, another experience to process. We never come to the end of infinite love, mercy, forgiveness, redemption, calling, and mission. We continue to pray to know God's will because God's will is always ahead of us—beckoning us. Following is the second step in walking with a formed heart; a step made up of millions of real steps, from the time we decide to look at life in a new way (repent) until the time we move from this world into the next. And perhaps even our entrance into heaven will continue the growth process we begin here on earth.

The third step in walking with a formed heart is instruction. Finally, we are at the place where the Sermon on the Mount begins (Matt. 5:1). Those who gathered to hear Jesus were the ones who were willing to look at life in a new way and believed that he could help them see what that new life looked like. The words of the Sermon on the Mount can penetrate our souls if we come with two prior experiences: looking at life in a new way and following Jesus into a lifelong process of discovery. Only then are we are ready to hear Jesus' words and respond to the message.

When we pray to know God's will, we submit to the ongoing instruction of the risen Christ given to us through the Holy Spirit (John 16:13-15). One basic meaning of the word *disciple* is "learner," and learning implies a recognition on our part that we need to be taught, coupled with a willingness to submit ourselves to the instructional process. Without this, even our initial repentance and our following will deteriorate. A generation of churchianity where membership has eclipsed discipleship bears witness to our need for instruction. We misunderstand Christianity and our place in it when our faith and experience lies behind us rather than ahead of us.

Thankfully, the witness of Christian history shows that such truncated Christianity has not always been the norm. It would astound our predecessors in the faith to know that we can become members and remain members of the church without ongoing formation. They would look with astonishment as confirmation[5] has deteriorated from becoming a disciple to becoming a church member. Moreover, they would have no idea what the phrase "inactive member" means when laid alongside the gospel. They would rejoice in the renewal of instruction (catechesis pre-baptism) and maturation (spiritual formation post-baptism) taking place in the body of Christ today. This lifelong process makes "disciples" (Matthew 28:19).

Jesus implies this process when he speaks of being "born from above," even though we misinterpret it by emphasizing the *moment* of birth rather than acknowledging the process that birth initiates. The birth of a baby evokes great joy in family and friends. But the word *birth* implies growth. If babies were born but not nurtured into further life, we would view their birth as a tragedy not a triumph. An event meant to bring joy would bring enormous grief, sadness, and loss. What must God feel about any interpretation of the Christian faith that leaves men and women as spiritual infants—as those who fail to live as God intended due to lack of instruction. Before the close of the New Testament, the writer of Hebrews saw people who were stuck in this arrested stage, still needing milk when they should be eating solid food (5:12).

Praying to know God's will involves engaging ourselves in the never-ending formational process that God has in mind for us. The effect of this commitment is to put an end to our thinking "what's the least I can do and still be a Christian" and replace it with "how far can I go in my walk with Christ with the remaining time I have left to live." The instructional process is initially a motivational shift. But with that in place, we find the height, depth, breadth, and length of God's knowledge and wisdom can keep us engaged as long as we live on this earth. The Dutch Reformed minister Andrew Murray wrote in the late nineteenth century about being "with Christ in the school of prayer," and that school is always in session!

The school offers instruction that helps form us into Christlikeness. Some today do not like to speak of formation in terms of Christlikeness because it seems too otherworldly and unattainable. But it is the language of scripture and tradition and the image Jesus gave us in John 15 as he invited us to "abide" in him and he in us. Paul invited the people he came in contact with to be "in Christ." Discerning prayer always relates to the ways and means to be more and more like Jesus, and Paul reveals these characteristics as the fruit of the Spirit (Gal. 5:22-23). When these nine dimensions are in place, we then work on the myriad of manifestations that flow from them. We are in Christ's school to learn more and more about his mind, his heart, and his work. We do this as individuals and as congregations.

It is important to remember that the entire formative process is ultimately for the sake of others. Our communion with Christ becomes compassion. Acts of piety ignite acts of mercy. The Spirit creates in us eyes and ears and, on the basis of what we have seen and heard, we witness and serve. Transformational discipleship (a gospel that has changed us) becomes a vocational discipleship (a gospel that seeks to offer Christ for the changing of others). We gain no greater joy and sense of fulfillment than in learning that the daily rounds and routines of our lives are the primary ways in which the gospel reaches the world.

I was reminded of living for Christ in the ordinary events of our lives when a men's group in Orlando invited me to speak. The group met on a Wednesday evening with the usual dinner and program format. The person who had invited me to speak asked me to talk about "vocational discipleship." I used Jesus' invitation to the first apostles to illustrate our using vocation as a means of grace to reach the world. At the close of the meeting, one man stayed behind to talk. In essence he said, "I have been a member of this church since I was a confirmed, and I have been a practicing lawyer in this city for twenty-five years. But tonight is the first time I have put being a church member and being a lawyer together. I will go to my law office in the morning for the first time as a conscious disciple of Jesus Christ."

This man had separated membership from discipleship. He had separated intake from outflow. He was in his mid-fifties and had yet to be instructed (or at least to "hear" the message) that his daily practice of law was the precise way God had called him to live out his commitment to Christ. Until then, he had been a disciple largely at church. Now, he would be a disciple for the world. I could tell by the look in his eye and the tone of his voice that he would arise the next day and look at his life in a different way. This new perspective reflects instruction in Christlikeness.

Earlier in the book, I referred to Frank Laubach's practice of beginning each day praying to know how he could connect his work with God's will. This is what the Orlando lawyer discovered, and it is essentially what it means for us to pray to know God's will. God is working in the world in ways that do not require our involvement.

God is always doing more than we can directly engage in. But this prayer also promotes the idea that we can take part in some of the work God is doing in the world today—work that we are supposed to be part of! At the intersection of God's will and our abilities, the Christian life comes alive! Where are you going tomorrow? What will you do there? Do it for Jesus! Praying to know God's will entails (to a great degree) getting up and doing what we normally do but now doing it consciously for Christ.

Repenting, following, and being instructed—three key steps in walking with a formed heart. All three steps relate to prayer. Because of the incessant resistance of our egotism, we need to pray, "God, help me to look at life the way you want me to look at it. I repent." Because the Christian life is a journey, we need to pray, "God, move out ahead of me and help me to go where you lead. I am your follower." And because our discipleship is shaped and deepened by instruction, we need to pray, "God, teach me whatever you want me to know at this time in my life, so I can grow in your grace. I am your student." This is praying to know the will of God. This is discernment. This is walking with a formed heart.

Questions for Reflection and Discussion

- Which "step" in walking with a formed heart spoke most to you? Why?
- What "new thing" is God teaching you?
- How do you sense God is leading you in discipleship?

Chapter 5

WALKING WITH A GUIDED HEART: SCRIPTURE

I grew up before the advent of television. The world didn't open up to me on a screen; it opened on a page. Reading a book unlocked life, exposing me to people, places, and things near and far away. Through reading I learned I was part of something larger and grander than myself or simply what I could see around me. Reading expanded my mind, stirred my emotions, and broadened my horizons. Reading gave me access to the wisdom of the ages, and it provided the motivation to apply that wisdom to my life. In many respects I am who I am today because of what I have read.

We have laid the foundation for discernment. With open and formed hearts, we stand poised for guidance.

The primary guide is the Bible. We are called to "take and read."[6] One early insight about praying to know God's will comes when we realize that much of God's will has already been given to us in scripture. We do not have to wait for the revelation we seek; it is there to be found. God calls us to walk with a guided heart through reading. And just as I experienced the expansion of my world as a child by reading, we also find our understanding of God's will widened and deepened by our exposure to scripture.

We seek not merely the reading of scripture but an encounter with it. We go beyond Bible study to live out what we read there. We read the Bible in ways that give rise to life in Christ. Our predecessors called this experience sapiential theology—a Christian life that both believes and behaves, professes and practices the faith. But how are we to garner this experience? The answer comes in *lectio divina*—a way of reading and praying the scriptures that Christians have used from at least the third century CE, and probably even earlier. In this chapter we will begin considering *lectio divina* as a way to progress on the journey into knowing and doing the will of God. I will tell of my personal discovery of *lectio divina* and my experience in practicing it. This chapter will not spell out the *lectio* process in detail. Suggested resources in the reading list at the end of the book will help in that area. Here we will take only two steps toward connecting *lectio divina* to the discernment process.

We take **the first step** when we view *lectio* as a way of praying the scriptures. That's why it fits into a book about praying to know God's will. Our predecessors in the faith knew that prayer embeds biblical revelation and activates it in our lives. So, *lectio divina* was never merely an act of reading. It is prayerful reading—reading with an open heart in the spirit of an ancient prayer, "Give me a word that I may live." This word is precisely what we seek when praying to know God's will. We search for a word of life—a word that leads us from being wanderers to being pilgrims, from darkness to light. As we survey the basic process of *lectio divina*, we will discover it as a form of prayer that begins, runs through, and ends the entire reading process.

This discovery transformed me. Reading the Bible has always served as my primary means for growing as a Christian. In fact, I could (and still can) get lost in scripture. The reading alone had negatively affected my devotional life; I would plan a time to both read and pray, only to realize I had spent all the time reading. My prayer life suffered as I tried to rush through a list of intercessions far too fast and superficially. I found the endeavor frustrating.

And then I learned that early Christians and many others since have never separated reading and praying. From the moment they opened the Bible, they were praying. Since prayer is always a response to God, what better time to pray than while we listen to God's voice in scripture? As soon as we turn to the reading for the day, we are receivers from the God who speaks and shows divine truth to us, and who, in that revelation, invites us to enter the text and give ourselves to it. Once I understood this invitation, my devotional life changed.

I no longer compartmentalized or categorized. All was prayer—prayer in response to scripture and then prayer in relation to life situations. From start to finish—prayer! We walk with a guided heart using *lectio divina* because it is a way of praying.

We take **a second step** by acknowledging that *lectio* creates a multifaceted spirit that further enriches our devotional life in general and our desire for discernment in particular. It produces the spirit of attentiveness. Rather than reading quantitatively, I began to read qualitatively. The Bible has the potential to change us with a single word or verse. While we can make good use of suggested reading plans, the point of reading scripture is not to follow a plan but to discover a Person.

Lectio released me to see that even though I might read a prescribed amount each day, I did not have to do so. I could freely choose to stop, look, and listen whenever prompted by the Spirit. I could read deeply, not just broadly. Words and phrases came alive in this kind of reading, because I gave myself permission to pay attention to them rather than feeling obligated to complete a certain amount of content. I had no daily-reading box to check, so my reading became more relaxed. *Lectio* gave me an attentiveness for the word.

Lectio also produced a spirit of engagement. Set free from the more-is-better approach, I could dig into those words and ideas that struck me, spoke to my mind, or warmed my heart. I did not have to move on. I could walk around a passage, spend time with it, and savor it.[7] I could bring forth previous knowledge I had about the passage and make use of resources that would shed new light upon it. Using this approach, I began to see the multiple layers of biblical meaning. In terms of discernment, this engagement revealed that praying to know God's will requires an unhurried embrace of the message. God wants to guide us through the whispers of grace (the nuances), not just the shouts (big-picture insights). *Lectio* created a disposition of the heart to pay attention to scripture and to look for the God-word in the word of God.

I found this meditative process extremely significant. Many times before, my eyes would pass over the words, but if anyone asked me, "What are you reading?" I could not tell them. I was preoccupied—distracted from the message the words were trying to send. I would come to the end of a Bible-reading time having completed the assigned amount for the day but feeling as if I had missed the point of the reading. I felt the Bible contained an ancient message—a message hard to understand and detached from my life today. *Lectio divina* saved me from that frustration. It liberated me to pay attention and then to engage in whatever caught my eye because the message was meant to transfer from the *then* of the Bible into the *now* of my daily living. *Lectio divina* expanded my reading from the cognitive *what* to the behavioral *so what.*

This freedom brought with it a spirit of responsiveness. I began to read the Bible the way I would read a letter or an e-mail from a friend. I looked forward to each reading because my heart was now exclaiming, "This is for me!" Of course, every passage has a historical context, and we need to know that original setting lest we begin to imagine things in the Bible that are not there. *Lectio divina* never diminishes the need for biblical study. It only reminds us that knowing the original context serves as the prelude to allowing the words that influenced that context to influence us. At this stage, we are not merely reading the Bible, we are beginning to let it read us! God is moving "into the neighborhood" (John 1:14, THE MESSAGE) and doing so with a revelation for *us*. Reading the Bible in this way can make us willing responders to God's word.

We will never know God's will unless and until we eagerly respond to it. Discernment is predicated on responsiveness. Otherwise, God's guidance rolls off our souls like water off a duck's back. Responsiveness opens the door so the risen Christ can come and converse with us. Responsiveness opens the windows so the wind of the Spirit can blow afresh into our lives. Look again at the ancient prayer—"Give me a word that I may live!"—and sense the spirit of responsiveness it evokes. To connect this with our learning from the last chapter, *lectio divina* is a form of repentance—a willingness to look at life from God's point of view, along with the disposition to put into practice what we discover.

Responsiveness led me to a spirit of integration. Like great music whose pattern runs through all the movements, the message found through *lectio* ran through all the dimensions of my life. Reading and praying scripture was no longer a "religious act"; it was a life practice. With the doors of my soul unlocked, God freely moved into any room of my spiritual house. With the windows of my soul opened, the wind of the Spirit was free to blow into any part of my spiritual house. Knowing God's will became a venture that could, on any given day, address any aspect of my life. In fact, over time I came to realize there were no categories—only a singular life meant to move under God's influence. *Lectio divina* revealed that the written word of God is the living Word of God (see Hebrews 4:12), moving into every area of our lives, affecting us comprehensively.

Once again, we see the connection between *lectio divina* and praying to know the will of God. We need God's guidance in the details, not just in the headlines. We desire to open ourselves to the influence of the Spirit upon our littleness, not just our largeness. *Lectio divina* enables us to accept God's message without trying to measure its significance. The smallest revelation is holy, because it comes to us from the living God. One step in the right direction is a step of faith made in response to grace. The coming of the Spirit no longer has to blow me away to have an effect.[8]

The final spirit created by *lectio* is action—living the message in my world and in my way. It is the Bible enacted; revelation performed. We're back to sapiential theology—believing and behaving. It is what the word *obedience* actually means: listening with the intention of putting into practice what we hear. We return to the inclination of our hearts, the disposition of our being to find and follow the will of God. *Lectio divina* is nothing other than praying to know God's will. And it occurs in all sorts of ways and settings.

This is why we can be in a small group and two people will read the same passage and draw different conclusions about converting the words into action. *Lectio divina* leads us to action but one tailored to our personality and to the unique situation in which we find ourselves. The Holy Spirit blows the word into our spiritual house and moves the curtains and cools the rooms. It turns the pages of the book that sits on the table and calls for the specific implementation that our present life situation creates. In the final analysis, discernment is praying in a way that leads to our taking action. Without action, we become barren fig trees that have trunks and limbs but no fruit.

In a practical sense, this is why any occasion of Bible reading must end with one or more questions like these:

- Is there a warning for me to heed?
- Is there a promise for me to embrace?
- Is there a specific way for me to put this message into action?
- Is there someone with whom I need to share what I have received?
- Is there somewhere I am going today that gives me the opportunity to put this message into practice?

Lectio divina transforms life through our performance of concrete actions. In this way, we reflect the spirit of James who exhorted his readers to be doers of the word, not hearers only (James 1:22).

We have explored the basic process of *lectio divina* in the preceding description of its substance and spirit. Classic *lectio divina* involves four "movements"—reading (*lectio*), meditating (*meditatio*), praying (*oratio*), and contemplation (*contemplatio*). More recent versions of *lectio* understand prayer (*oratio*) as the piece that encircles the entire experience, with *lectio, meditatio,* and *contemplatio* giving shape to the element of *actio* (performance).[9] But as I said at the beginning, this chapter is not a study of *lectio divina* but an invitation into the experience of it, particularly as praying the Bible becomes a divinely ordained means of knowing and doing God's will.

We read (*lectio*) the Bible slowly and attentively, so that a portion of it may strike us and draw our attention. We walk around that selected passage (*meditatio*) using all our faculties and tools to probe it and benefit from it. We embrace the message (*contemplatio*), so that the written word becomes the living word in us. And then, we enact the message (*actio*), so that our lives become instruments of God's grace in the routines of our everyday living. In this way, we walk with a guided heart. Our praying to know God's will is transformed into the doing of it. We become agents who incarnate the Lord's Prayer: "Thy kingdom come. Thy will be done in earth, as *it is* in heaven" (Matt. 6:10, KJV).

If I could come to you and bless you, I would come with a prayer asking God to create this sense of wonder in you as you approach the Bible. I would ask God to use scripture to broaden and deepen your sense of reality and where you fit into it. I'm old enough to remember the effect of reading upon me when I was a child. I pray you are young enough to recapture it in your spiritual formation. Open the Bible; prayerfully read it; and allow the Spirit to reveal how you are to become a living witness to its message. Walk with a guided heart.

Questions for Reflection and Discussion

- Which part of the *lectio divina* process spoke to you most? Why?
- How does responsiveness enhance your discernment?
- How do you read the Bible with a sense of wonder?

Chapter 6

WALKING WITH A GUIDED HEART: TRADITION

Once in a while I imagine what it might have been like to be the first person to have a particular experience—a specific location, a type of food, or a moment in history. In my lifetime, the person that comes most quickly to mind is Neil Armstrong, the first human being to set foot on the moon. Decades later, I still find watching the old black-and-white video a moving experience. Astronaut Armstrong not only accomplished a remarkable feat; he also joined a comparatively tiny group of people who actually do something before anyone else.

Most of us go places and do things after others have been there or done that. And for the most part, we usually come later with the benefits of the first person and those who followed. We come to our moment here or there with this or that, doing so with an enrichment due to those who came before us. Some of the first-timers improved the surroundings; others wrote about their discoveries. We come along and enjoy a better experience because of them.

Praying to know the will of God is one such experience. We are not the first people to seek God's will. Others have done so, and we can benefit from their learning. Their wisdom, counsel, and practice contribute to our discernment process. We call these benefits "the witness of the saints." And we have roughly two thousand years of Christian witness to draw upon. We may think we have to come fresh to God's will. But the fact is, much of God's will is already known.

Those who have preceded us can offer guidance. We considered guidance through scripture in the last chapter. In this chapter, we turn to tradition. If the Bible is "the book of God" (a phrase John Wesley liked), then tradition is "the book of the church" that sheds light on the original revelation. If the Bible is canon, tradition is commentary; together, the two reveal an enormous amount of God's will. Some of our confusion regarding discernment lies in the fact that we have not done our homework—we have not studied the records of scripture and tradition. Had we done so, we would pray less for discernment and pray more for grace to do God's will as others have done. So, in this chapter we will look at some of the steps we can take in relation to the Christian tradition to help us when we pray to know God's will.

First, there is **the step** of establishing roots. Tradition grafts us into an amazing family tree! We can include the biblical characters on that tree, but in this chapter we will consider the men and women who have lived between the close of the Bible and today. If nothing else, we discover that our desire to know and do the will of God runs through the entirety of the Judeo-Christian tradition. Every generation of Christians has prayed, "Thy will be done," just as we do. It comes to us with all the insights that the praying of it bestows.

We see, for example, the insights coming from a wide variety of faith traditions: Roman Catholic, Eastern Orthodox, and Protestant (mainline and nondenominational). From the saints who have recorded their experiences and their teachings we gain further insight into our own praying, not only of the Lord's Prayer in particular but also of the practice of prayer in general. We see discernment employed in the context of corporate worship, in the midst of small-group meetings, and in times of private devotion. We see some of our predecessors using prayer books and liturgy to discern the will of God; we find others speaking their desire to know God's will in unknown tongues. We watch them finding and following God's will in different time frames and diverse cultures. Every time we capture one new thought or are inspired by one new example, our roots are strengthened. Just as a healthy tree develops a richer life by a wider reach, so also our spiritual formation is enriched by exposure to the saints of the ages.

Over the course of my life, I have often heard Christians refer to their desire to "live a deeper Christian life." I have said the same and sought it. But in the last twenty years or so, I have begun to respond to another desire within me: the desire to "live a *broader* Christian life." This new desire set me on a pilgrimage to find out what I can learn from people who pray differently than I do, rather than limiting myself to the examples of people who pray the way I usually do. This igniting of a "holy experimentation" allows me to express my thoughts, feelings, and words through means that were not part of West Texas Methodism. Like every other person, I still have my preferences and patterns. But I also have a growing wealth of viable options that enable me to pray better in general and to discern better in particular. I choose to take the step of developing good roots as I avail myself of the witness of the saints and the insights of tradition.

The second step is the step of realism. We do not even leave the Bible and move into tradition without coming in contact with the blood of the martyrs (see Hebrews 11)—to say nothing of Jesus' sufferings and those of the priests and prophets who preceded him. We learn early on that the Christian life will be marked by successes and failures, pleasures and pains, advances and setbacks—what the tradition calls consolations and desolations. When we connect this understanding with praying to know God's will, we will not evaluate our discernment by how "positive" it is. Praying to know God's will expresses itself across the full range of emotions; discovering God's will comes to us through all of life.

My study of John Wesley has helped me. In his private diaries, Wesley used a code system to monitor his spiritual temperament. With respect to prayer, it ranged from "cold and indifferent" to "warm and effectual" based on the placement of a line and the letter *p* in his recordings in his diary. If the line was above the letter, he considered his praying "warm and effectual." If the line ran through the middle of the letter, he assessed his praying to be average. If he placed the line below the letter, he deemed his prayers to be "cold and indifferent."

When I first noted Wesley's system, I immediately connected with it because it reflects the way my own praying seems to be. Some days "warm and effectual" but other days "cold and indifferent." Most days, like Wesley's, the line falls somewhere between these extremes. This kind of prayer is realistic. I took encouragement from the diary markings of a man considered to be a true saint of God, but one who experienced and monitored the same kind of fluctuations in prayer that I see in my praying.

Even more, I noticed that the letter *p* did not disappear from Wesley's diary. Whether his prayers were hot, average, or cold—he kept praying. The authenticity of prayer does not rely on its level of emotion but rather on its genuineness of communion. This perspective on prayer has radically altered the way I view the practice of it. And it has also affected those times when I pray to know God's will. I realize that such praying will span the spectrum. Yes, I will know moments of discernment when I feel my heart "strangely warmed."[10] I also perceive that sometimes my cry to know God's will results in a sense that God has moved and left no forwarding address.

But like Wesley and so many others, I keep praying regardless of how I feel in the moment. Thankfully, my exposure to the breadth of the Christian tradition has confirmed this same realism. One after another, the saints of the ages line up, join hands, and reveal that praying to know God's will has always been a mixed bag of emotions and experiences. But they kept praying and, as the writer of Hebrews put it (12:1), those saints surround me like a great cloud, and their witness is clear: "Don't stop! Stay at it!"

The great gift of realism is joy. Whether the will of God comes to me as a pleasant or painful reality, it comes wrapped in joy. How can this be? I recognize that joy resides in the finding and the following rather than in the emotional atmosphere that attends the doing of it. Again, tradition comes to my assistance. I can read the story of real men and women who endured great trials but did so with joy—including being killed (sometimes slowly and painfully) because of their faith in Christ. Their example does not make my praying morbid; it makes it genuine. Joy comes in knowing and doing the will of God, not in the manner in which I live out that will. Christ's own experience bears this out.

The third step on the journey of tradition is relevance. By this I mean reading something written by one of the saints and having the sense that "this is for me!" Words that may have been written nearly two thousand years ago are suddenly as real as if they had been sent to me in a personal communication. Without warning, the minds and hearts of Christian predecessors provide guidance for some aspect of my life. They may have written with a quill pen, but I receive the message in a cyberspace world.

The space between them and me is almost nil; it seems as if they are sitting right where I am. In a mysterious way, their knowing God's will enables me to know what it is. Far from being old, dusty words written in the long ago and far away, the writings of Christian predecessors preserved by Christian tradition are the means God chooses to speak to me. The words ring with truth and convey an air of relevance. That's one reason I now read from the devotional classics each day.

I will give one example from the conferences of John Cassian.[11] The second conference deals specifically with discernment, what Cassian and others have called "discretion." I hope the following points will confirm the richness of the classics in general, while illustrating that the saints can shed great light on the subject of discernment.

1. Discernment is the root and source of the virtues, otherwise good things can be used for the wrong motives.

2. Without discernment, falls from grace are inevitable. Conference Two cites examples from a number of biblical characters.

3. Discernment exists in humility. The person seeking to know God's will always submits the revelation to the elders. No one acts out the will of God independently and certainly not arrogantly.

4. Discernment avoids extremes. This applies both to the practices that attend praying for discernment (e.g., extreme fasting), as well as the actions that express the discernment.

These four insights barely scratch the surface of Cassian's second conference, but they show us how specific the classics can be.

For decades I have taught the simple phrase "spirituality is reality." I have tried to communicate my conviction that the establishment and maintenance of the Christian spiritual life is not the result of speculation or the application of abstract principles. Instead, I believe we see the will of God in the lives of men and women who have faced each day just as we do. Some of these people are living, and others have been dead for centuries. But their witness and wisdom provide the basis for confidence that we are in the ballpark when it comes to knowing and doing God's will. Their counsel will strike us as relevant to the situations we face. We still have to wrestle with knowing how to apply their counsel, but we will engage that struggle with an assurance that we have been given truth that can be lived.

As you pray to know the will of God, I hope that you will include the witness of the saints in your discernment process. A great cloud of witnesses surrounds us still. Though many have died, they speak living words that God uses to communicate the divine will for our lives today. I do not know how it works, but I hope that my arrival in heaven will include the opportunity to look some of them up and say thank you. I could not be the Christian I am today had it not been for them, and neither could you!

Questions for Reflection and Discussion

- Who are the saints in the "great cloud of witnesses" who help you?
- How is your Christian life broader, not just deeper?
- How do the saints help you keep your faith real?

Chapter 7

WALKING WITH A GUIDED HEART: COMMUNITY

Years ago I faced a major decision that had implications for my entire family and one that would necessitate a move. In my reflection time I kept going back and forth. One day I felt that I should say yes to the opportunity, and the next day I felt I should say no. Fortunately, I was meeting each week with other faculty colleagues. Over time we had grown to be deep friends, and we had helped one another figure things out on multiple occasions. Naturally I spoke of my situation to the group. I knew they would speak the truth in love to me, no matter what they thought. The group's collective wisdom resolved my personal confusion and their collective love strengthened my confidence to make the right decision. In the end, it meant having to say good-bye to the very friends who helped me make the decision. But even in the parting there was joy, because we believed the decision to accept the invitation was God's will.

Is the word *church* singular or plural? It depends on whether we ask an English teacher or a theologian. English teachers will tell us it's singular, and grammatically that is correct. The plural form is "churches." But a theologian will always tell us that "church" is plural. There is no one-member church. We are part of the body of Christ, taking our place as individual members of it—in connection and union with all other Christians who are part of it as well. When we think of the church in any other way, we fall prey to a privatized spirituality.

Similarly, we always practice discernment in community—in concert with the insights that other believers contribute to our desire to know and do God's will. We began our look at the corporate dimension of discernment in the last chapter as we reminded ourselves that tradition guides us. This chapter continues the same theme but moves it into the present and into the guidance afforded us by other believers in our relationship network. This includes members of our congregation but can extend beyond the local church to friends who walk the journey with us from afar.

Most of us are part of denominations or associations that are larger than a local congregation. Their heritage enriches our praying to know God's will. Ecclesial bodies have accumulated wisdom that we access and apply to our benefit. Just as we need to read the Bible to find what

God has already revealed, we also need to explore the history and insight of our faith tradition.

Having ministered in the church and in theological education for more than forty years, I have seen the difference between persons who have been "traditioned" and those who practice their faith as freelance Christians. The difference is one of perspective: the sense of moving in a stream of wisdom that has been flowing for a long time, versus the sense of making it up as we go along. It is the difference between a flower growing in a garden and one stuck in a vase. They both look the same. But the one in the vase is dying. As a cut flower it lacks roots into the nourishment that keeps it alive.

The earliest Christians had to deal with cut-flower people. The *Didache* warned against false prophets who wandered from place to place, never "rooting" themselves in a group of believers or becoming accountable to any authority other than themselves. About five centuries later, Saint Benedict warned against the Sarabaites, those monks who lived without a Rule to guide them, no previous experience to inform them, and no community to hold them accountable. Added to this, some of them were mentally and emotionally unstable, becoming real "loose cannons" on the deck of the ship called the church.[12] Unfortunately, the pages of church history have continued to include men and women who functioned as "independent Christians," usually inflicting harm on the church as they did so.

John Wesley observed people in his day who were cut-flower Christians. He called them "holy solitaries," and he did not use that term as a compliment! Rather, he used it to describe Christians who are separated from the guidance of tradition and from the counsel of members of the body of Christ. Wesley was delineating the qualities of a pseudospirituality—a "me and Jesus" faith that may look good but is dying. And even worse, it may turn out to be spiritual wax fruit. When we apply these concerns to discernment, we gain a sense in which we never say, "God told me . . . ," for if God tells us something, it will connect and conform to some portion of the Christian faith. So, we turn our attention in this chapter to the guidance that comes to us through Christian community, using our life together to reveal significant steps on our journey to know God's will.

Our first step in benefiting from communal guidance is to realize that it comes to us in different forms. The fundamental form is **one-to-one guidance**, which we usually refer to as spiritual friendship or spiritual direction. We receive counsel from a trusted friend, wise disciple, or trained director—someone who has walked the path and will speak the truth in love to us. The experience may come through conversations or from more formal engagements. The time together remains focused and personal. Neither one amends the agenda or makes it more generic. This form of guidance can be tailor-made to our journey. It is not selfish; it is specific. We have a soulprint just as we have fingerprints. We require unique guidance that applies to the situations we face.

The second form of communal guidance is **one-to-group**. We join others in seeking a spiritual guide who can give us collective insight. We form a small group around someone whom we feel can help us find and follow God's will. This "direction in common" has less personal expression. Our sharing issues and themes with other believers increases the value of this input to our formation. A wise guide can meet with a group to provide help on the general life of discipleship. In the course of participation, we (as members of the group) can garner beneficial insights from one another. Methodism's classes and bands illustrate the value of this level of community discernment. In the Wesleyan tradition, John and Charles Wesley provided this level of guidance through their visits to United Societies and through their letters.

A third form is **group-to-one**. In this kind of guidance, an individual receives input from many people. It can occur as we seek more than one opinion on a particular matter. We can receive guidance by collecting advice from trusted friends. It can also occur as we submit ourselves to an established group of people and receive their counsel. I think of the process in which clergy candidates meet periodically with established groups and are given guidance that moves them on to ordination. It also happens when someone asks to be placed on the agenda of a board meeting to gain formal approval and implementation of an idea. We make use of this kind of community guidance when we want to integrate ourselves into the life of an established body of people. Again, early Methodism used this kind of discernment in the annual conference.

Group-to-group guidance provides the final form of communal guidance. We see this most often when a number of people approach another body, asking its opinion or approval. A new small group needs permission to meet in a room in the church. Or perhaps a renewal group is seeking to integrate itself into the larger church. Denominations experience group-to-group guidance when multiple congregations meet each year (such as annual conference) or when they meet every four years (for example, the General Conference of The United Methodist Church). This kind of guidance usually comes about related to "official" and "binding" decisions. It represents the most formal way of determining where our sense of God's will fits into the existing principles and practices of the Christian church.

All these types of communal guidance are means of grace, expressions of what John Wesley called Christian Conferencing. For him and those in the Anglo-Catholic traditions, this conferencing was part of the Instituted Means of Grace (works of piety) that Christ himself had initiated and his followers had carried on. We need to remember this fact, lest we get the idea that a personal revelation from the Spirit is more "spiritual" than one mediated through a secondary source. And it prevents us from thinking that a private revelation always takes precedence over a communal one. By keeping communal guidance within the means of grace, we remember that God speaks to us directly and indirectly—and seldom without some combination of the two.

With the basic forms of community guidance in mind we are ready to take the second step, the step of facilitation. We do this in relation to the initiation of the process and the environment in which it occurs. I can describe the matter of initiation simply. When one-to-one guidance or one-to-group guidance is called for, the person who desires it will initiate the experience. True spiritual guides do not approach us with an offer to help. Instead, they wait for us to ask them for guidance. This requires initiative on our part as seekers, and it calls for humility on the part of the guide. Both the seeker and the guide function in relation to the promptings of the Holy Spirit.

When the form of community guidance is group-to-one or group-to-group, the initiation may come from either side of the relationship. The choice of time and place usually falls to the discretion of the larger group. Those who seek guidance will be placed on the agenda, and the discernment conversation will take place during the regularly scheduled meeting. Additional meetings may be necessary, but the process will usually begin within the already established meeting schedule of the group. Even when the desired guidance is particularly sensitive, it can begin this way as the larger group goes into "executive session" to preserve the confidentiality of the guidance process.

In both types of facilitation, the environment of the discernment relies on trust that God's will can be found through consensus. This is not a time for a regulatory (such as Robert's Rules of Order) approach.[13] The will of God is not often discerned by waiting until 51% of the group can agree. Frequently, God's will surfaces through the insights of the minority. So, the environment is not one of "voting" but "uniting" to find and follow God's will.

Furthermore, the environment of community guidance is that of "we are in this together." We are not competitors. We are in search of the will of God.

This approach implies that the people whose views do not ultimately prevail will yield to the consensus of the group. There are no sore losers or after-meetings in the parking lot or over the telephone. What's done is done. The entire group lives with the assumption that it has found the will of God and now will follow it. This environment of submission bases its procedure on the trust that the common mind is usually more correct than the individual perception. Assuming the group has discerned God's will also means that the members trust the Holy Spirit to reveal further insight to support revisions.

Having chosen the form of guidance best suited for our purposes and having established a healthy environment for it, we take a third step in the community-guidance process: the step of paying attention to "red flags" that can pop up along the way. In general, this step involves the recognition that matters can arise in the midst of discernment to confuse and mislead even a well-intentioned process. Failure to acknowledge such red flags can lead to arrogance on the one hand (making discernment a pride-filled and presumptuous experience) or to ignorance on the other hand (making discernment an almost totally subjective process). Paying attention to red flags keeps us attentive and realistic in the community discernment process. Because community guidance is experienced in a wide variety of ways, we can explore only a few selected red flags this chapter. They exemplify issues to watch for as we seek to find and follow God's will together.

One of the main flags comes when a church thinks that an action has to be "in the manual" to be of God. This assumption makes discernment a regulated experience rather than a relational one. It assumes that the will of God has somehow been previously predicted, recorded, and codified. So, rather than turning to the Holy Spirit, the group turns to actual guidelines (such as meeting minutes and program manuals) and tries to make the future conform to the past. Sometimes, this approach can become more complicated as outspoken, control-oriented persons use their "past memories" as if they were definitive of both current and future reality.

This reliance on guidelines and memory raises a serious flag for corporate discernment, and it is a tricky one to navigate. Obviously, some truths have been revealed in scripture and tradition. We are not free to radically change such matters. But we are free to interpret them to our time and place prayerfully and carefully. Even in relation to abiding truths we ask, "How then shall we live in relation to these things?" We hold to the will of God as we have received it, while recognizing that the present discernment process may need to enact that will in fresh ways. To miss this flag is to fall prey to the old adages, "We've never done it that way before" or "Don't confuse me with the facts; my mind is already made up." When we confront the red flag of lock-step conformity to the past, we allow the wind of the Spirit to blow into the current discernment process.

A second flag arises when we think that we can have gains without losses. Failure to recognize this flag means the group may fall prey to "death by addition." It can happen to individuals and to congregations who come to believe the worldview that bigger is better, more is better, and so on. Instead, the community guidance process includes asking, "What do we need to let go of in order to embrace the new thing God is calling for?" God's new direction is not meant to be the straw that breaks the camel's back. And in many cases, too few people in the church already carry too much of the load. Moving forward in discernment is not trying to squeeze more blood out of the turnips! Wise spiritual guides and mature discernment committees know that we must let go of some things in order to grasp the will of God for our future.

A third flag pops up when we allow a single person or even a cliquish small group to say, "We speak for everyone." This flag hijacks group discernment by allegation rather than by reality. From the outset, we know that God's will is always found in the midst of variations and multiple viable options. Rarely do we have only one possible way to enact the will of God. So, it is not healthy to conduct group discernment with a "this is the only way" mentality. High-control individuals must not be allowed to take their personal opinions and make them appear to be universal. Wise discernment committees will receive personal opinions with appreciation and then say, in effect, "We will be checking this out in the coming days to be sure we are moving with the widest possible perspective." If the church is large enough and has enough personnel, the community guidance process may result in more than one enactment. But whether we can do God's will in one way or in many, we will not allow the red flag of alleged universality to define the discernment process.

This brief list of flags is largely nonfunctional. Most community guidance does not fail in determining action steps as much as it fails at a deeper level—the layers that have to do with motives and presuppositions. The main flags to get rid of are those that block the communication process, those that keep the conversation superficial or safe, and those that make the process appear to be one of discernment when it is really only a smoke-and-mirrors experience until the dominant individual or group gets its way. Discernment best occurs in an atmosphere where no one presumes in advance to know the will of God. This is the spirit of the Lord's Prayer (and all prayer, for that matter); otherwise, we would never have to pray "thy will be done" because someone in the room would already know it!

As we bring this chapter to a close, we must return to the underlying principles that form the foundation for community guidance. The main one is simply that God wants to reveal the divine will more than we want to know it. We are not rolling the dice nor are we at the mercy of random impressions. When we take the revelation of scripture, the insights of tradition, and the wisdom of a praying community (made up of healthy and devoted Christ followers), we have a lot going for us. The Holy Spirit stops us just short of equating our ideas with

God's will. Praying to know God's will is always an act of personal and corporate humility. But it is also a process based upon the confidence that we are in communion with the God who speaks and shows.

In the end we are not seeking a special program or plan—we are seeking God. God ultimately wills that we establish and maintain a relationship between our spirit and the Holy Spirit. Everything else flows from that—including those painfully protracted periods when no one really knows God's will. When we ally with God, we do not have to be in a hurry. We do not have to feel pressured or pushed to get something done fast. We may know what to do, or we may not. But either way, we know God. And until the discernment comes, the relationship satisfies. With this relational base, we pray to know God and experience less concern around knowing God's will. One thing we always affirm: God loves us and remains in control!

Questions for Reflection and Discussion

- What comes to your mind when you read that theologically the word *church* is plural?
- How does the idea of consensus inform your understanding of discernment?
- When have you faced any of the "red flags" in communal discernment? How did you deal with them? How did you learn from them?

Chapter 8

WALKING WITH A
SURRENDERED HEART

I met Jeannie on a blind date. I fell in love with her almost immediately. My love for her grew into desire for a lifelong relationship. I found that the greatest sign of my love was my desire to please her, to do the things she asked me to do. At the same time, I found that her love for me was rooted in the same desire. The mutual surrender of our lives to each other remains the essence of our love and the foundation of our relationship. I believe that the best word for understanding the foundation for praying to know God's will is *surrender*. We will explore it in this chapter.

We have been looking at concrete practices that can bring us into the spirit of discernment. We have seen how scripture, tradition, and community contribute to our ability to know and follow God's will. But all this practice and knowledge comes to naught if we have no desire to surrender ourselves to God as we pray to know and do God's will. Just as in our human relations, the divine-human relationship is marked by surrender. In this chapter we want to move outside the specifics of discernment and regain "the big picture" of it—walking with a surrendered heart.

We do this when we pray, "Thy kingdom come. Thy will be done in earth, as *it is* in heaven" (Matt. 6:10, KJV). We say, in effect, that we submit ourselves to being persons through whom God can work. We do not stand outside the circle of our own praying; we do not pass the buck to some spirit-being or to another human being. We say what Isaiah uttered so long ago, "Here am I; send me!" (6:8). To walk with a surrendered heart is to walk in humility and in the willingness to let our lives be instruments of God's grace. Praying to know God's will takes root in this desire.

I experienced a significant learning when I discovered that our predecessors in the faith named humility the primary evidence of the love of God in our heart. We see this most clearly in the first Beatitude, "Blessed are the poor in spirit" (Matt. 5:3). The spiritual life begins as we confess our radical need for God—our utter poverty in trying to live without God. The Christian faith begins in abandonment to God as the source of our life and work. This understanding has a direct bearing on praying to know God's will; nothing short-circuits discernment more than the lack of humility. We are never more in danger of missing God's will than when we approach our need for it with an arrogance that causes us to believe we have an "inside track" with God. And nothing can mess up a group discernment process more than having participants in the group who feel sure they know what God wants everyone else to do.

We must not base discernment in functionalism. I am convinced that discernment is the child born of spirit more than skill. It involves temperament more than technique. An attitude that can both search for and receive God's will when it is given precedes action that seeks discernment. That's what I describe as surrender. I see Paul calling for it in his words to the Roman Christians to "present your bodies . . . to God" (12:1). Walking in the light means walking with a surrendered heart. It reflects the disposition of abandonment to divine providence, which undergirds all we have been saying about praying to know God's will.

All this knowledge came together for me in an unexpected way. On my first visit to the Abbey of Gethsemani in the early 1980s, I literally walked under two words as I entered the Guest House: *God Alone.* I could not fail to see them, for they were chiseled in stone above the door. I had a general grasp of what the words meant. But what I had yet to learn—and what I only began partially to see in that first visit to the Abbey—was how the two words summarize the Christian tradition's belief in the necessity of surrender and how they express the monastic commitment to a life of devotion that reflects a surrendered heart. I am still on the journey of discovering one saint after another who lived and wrote about the "God

Alone" life. I believe it is one dimension of the abundant life Jesus spoke of in John 10:10. I also believe it is the essence of the Christian spiritual life and the spirit that precedes knowing the will of God. So, as in previous chapters, let's examine some steps we take in walking with a surrendered heart.

The first step, Paul says, is that we present our bodies to God. He means more than our physical bodies; he means our entire selves. He asks for a complete dedication of every part of our lives to God. The idea of presentation implies that we do so willingly. This takes me back to my new relationship with Jeannie. No one had to tell me to call her or to ask her out on subsequent dates. No one forced me to drive to her house and stop in for a visit. All of this, and more, came from deep within me—romance evolving into love. A power greater than myself grasped me, and I found it great fun to "present" myself to her.

Praying to know God's will constitutes an act of presentation on our part. We can write about it in a book, but no one forces us to do it. The desire to know and do God's will is the supreme joy of the Christian. We pray to know God's will because nothing seems more fulfilling than finding out what that will is and doing it—even when it is challenging or costly. When we walk with a surrendered heart of love, we do all this willingly.

Paul writes that we present ourselves. Many translations use the phrase "your bodies," and this surely indicates that true spirituality includes the tangible and the intangible—the flesh as well as the spirit. In fact, when Paul wrote these words, one of the biggest obstacles to the spiritual life in general and the Christian life in particular (as it was emerging in the Greco-Roman world) was a misuse of the body in self-gratification. Paul's exhortation for the Roman Christians to present their bodies to God was a radical idea but one essential to living the life God intended.

The same holds true for us in the life of discipleship. Praying to know God's will always issues in concrete expression. Our "bodies" are always the final conduits of our spirituality. Our faith moves hands and hearts, tongues and temperaments.

From within this approach arises the idea of uniqueness. No one can be "you" better than you can. We have been made by a creator God, not a cloning one. Your life is absolutely unique and unrepeatable. When we present ourselves to God, we offer to God the one-of-a-kind people that we are. Praying to know and do God's will may have similarities to that of others; but in the final analysis, no one can find and follow the will of God for our lives except us! Discernment is one of the most personal things we can experience, which makes it challenging (even scary) to engage in it. We like the security of blending into the crowd, of being invisible. But when God says, "Here is my will; do it," our only option is to be ourselves. Walking with a surrendered heart entails presenting ourselves to God as we realize that our soulprint is as unique as our fingerprint.

This principle applies to congregations as well as to individuals. No two churches are alike. Part of the ecclesial discernment process is to discover why God has put "us" where we are and to develop our mission accordingly. There are transferable concepts but no duplicates. We do not go to other churches in order to find our identity and mission. The first act of praying to know God's will as a congregation begins with pondering the phrase "the kingdom of heaven has come near." Locality and vocation have a strong connection.

Paul invokes **a second step**, the invitation to present ourselves to God as *living sacrifices*. To grasp the full impact of this phrase, we must think like Jews and others whose religion included the notion of sacrifice. And keeping that idea in mind, people in Paul's time would have been blown away by reading the words *living* and *sacrifice* in the same sentence. The only sacrifices people knew about were dead ones. But Paul invites us to be *living* sacrifices. What would that entail?

Simply put, it means that the will of God comes from the offering of our lives. The words of an old hymn capture the meaning, "Take my life, and let it be consecrated, Lord, to thee." Each stanza describes some aspect of life that becomes a means to express God's will in the world. In addition, a *living sacrifice* is one we can make again and again. A traditional sacrifice could only be made once. We can sacrifice to God daily. And that is the essence of the Christian life—thinking, saying, and doing God's will again and again and again. Only a living sacrifice can do that.

Living sacrifice also denotes our aliveness to the current moment. The pattern of God's will expresses itself in particulars. For example, if we believe that God wills us to love other people, we pray repeatedly about the expression of that will when specific people and situations cross our path. We can gain insight from the past, and our experiences are good teachers. But we can only *do* God's will one occurrence at a time. So, we must "practice the presence of God" (Brother Lawrence's phrase) in the context of the present moment.

In the first church I pastored, Jeannie and I were blessed to know Mrs. Parker. She was already advanced in age when we first met her. She rested on the borderline of being able to come to church and becoming a home-bound member. It didn't take us long to realize she was one of the church's true saints. Her countenance reflected Christ, and her wisdom was a gift to me as a young pastor.

In my last cycle of visits before moving to the next appointment, I went to Mrs. Parker's home. I asked her the same question I posed to everyone as I visited for the final time: "What spiritual lesson have you learned that has been a blessing to you?" After a brief pause, Mrs. Parker responded, "Well, I have learned that wherever I am, God is."

Knowing Mrs. Parker, I immediately realized that she had answered well, for that is the way she lived. In every moment of her life she stayed alive to the situation and to the ways she could be a living sacrifice for God in it. As the years have gone by, I have learned how many other saints have walked by the same conviction. Their lives are characterized as living sacrifices precisely because the present moment is their arena for living. Walking with a surrendered heart means walking as a living sacrifice.

To be a living sacrifice, Paul says, is a holy thing—
something acceptable to God, something pleasing to
God. Some translations have Paul saying that living this
way is our "spiritual worship," while others use the phrase
"reasonable service." I have always been struck by the fact
that the phrase in the Greek can mean either, which is
significant. God does not separate what we often separate—namely, our worship from our service. The Greek
word *latreia* carries both meanings. Our worship is an
act of service, and our service is an act of worship. When
we apply this cross reference to discernment, it suggests
that when we behave as living sacrifices we will worship/
serve and serve/worship as a singular expression. We will
never use discernment to divide personal gospel from
social gospel. As we pray to know the will of God, we
acknowledge that our lives will reflect differing aspects
of God's singular will. This remembrance prevents us
from chopping the will of God into pieces or allowing
one piece to compete with another one. This disposition
reminds us that the word *salvation* means "wholeness,"
and we do well to approach praying to know God's will
with the same reverence that we speak of in the service of
holy matrimony: "Those whom God has joined together,
let no one put asunder." In other words, praying to know
God's will is an act that allows God to do in us and through
us whatever gives honor and glory to God.

The third step is for us to shun conformity to the
world. For the Bible, one use of the word *world* summarizes
in one word all that opposes the will of God. As a result
of the Fall in Genesis 3, creation becomes "world." The

garden becomes a jungle, where human self-centeredness replaces God-centeredness. And the rest is history—literally. To walk with a surrendered heart is to walk toward God, not away from God. We move in ways that reduce self-sufficiency and increase God-dependency. We find ourselves less and less conformed to (shaped like) the world and more and more formed into the likeness of Christ.[14] Of course, this does not happen all at once, but the disposition of our heart sets the trajectory for our walk with God.

Interestingly, our refusal to be conformed to the world provides the incentive to "get up and start over" when we fail. Despair reflects the attitude of a person who has given up and given in, believing that the negative has won the day and simply resigning ourselves to it. But the spiritual life is not resignation; it is renunciation. We denounce the alleged truth that evil wins and cling tenaciously to the belief that God wins—that love triumphs. So, one dimension of praying to know God's will comes in refusing to settle for anything other than that will. We partake of the spirit of Brother Lawrence who, when asked what he did when he failed and fell, simply replied that he raised his arms to Jesus, who picked him up, set him on his feet, and got him moving again.[15] Sometimes, the prayer of discernment is our way of saying, "Satan, your will is not the last word in this situation; God's will is." That's what it means to no longer be conformed to the world.

This nonconformity does not leave us in limbo. Our detachment from the world is simultaneously our attachment to Christ. Our nonconformity to the world is our immediate and ongoing conformity to Christ. Discernment does not leave us empty, but rather provides the positive incentive and ingredients to reshape us into fully devoted followers of Jesus.

The fourth step flows from the third and comes with the renewing of our minds. This step serves as the means for bringing the first three into being. We are able, Paul says, to present ourselves to God as living sacrifices, renouncing the world, because our minds have been renewed. In this passage, he does not specifically define what this means, but the use of the word *mind* in his other writings offers a good basis for figuring it out.[16] For Paul, the mind goes beyond our rational faculties, although he includes them. Our mind represents the dominant disposition of our entire existence. We use the word in this way when we say, "I am of a *mind* to do that." When we put our mind into something, we are bringing all our energies to bear upon the matter at hand. Eugene Peterson captures the spirit of Paul's words in his translation of Romans 12:1 in *The Message.*

> So, here's what I want you to do, God helping you: Take your everyday, ordinary life—your sleeping, eating, going-to-work, and walking-around life— and place it before God as an offering.

We are back to "The Hokey Pokey"—back to the point of putting our whole selves (our minds) into the process of praying to know God's will. In other words, discernment is no halfhearted matter, no casual or superficial endeavor. We direct all our powers of observation and intention toward this one thing: finding and following God's will. Paul wrote of this even more eloquently in Philippians 2:5, when he urged his friends to have the same mind that was in Christ. Clearly Jesus had only one mind: to do the will of God. So, the mark of a renewed mind is the sole desire for our lives to be instruments through which God's will can be done on earth as it is in heaven.

When we take these four steps, Paul concludes that we will discern the will of God. He is not speaking of some outcome made possible by a mechanical action—no spiritual pulling a lever and getting the prize to drop out. But he is addressing our need to walk with a surrendered heart, approaching the praying to know God's will with the prior desire to do it. Does it always work? Of course not. But it places us in the vicinity of revelation, combining it with personal willingness to carry it out once we know it. Whether we find the will of God quickly or slowly, easily or with difficulty or sometimes not at all, we know we seek God's will with a heart already surrendered to it. Walking with a surrendered heart remains the constant in praying to know God's will.

With this thought in mind, I close this chapter with the prayer attributed to Saint Francis, who walked with a heart surrendered to God. God used Francis to promote the divine will in the world. Can we desire more than that? I invite us to use the following version of the prayer as a way of bringing this chapter to a close. I promise that I have done the same thing as I bring the writing of this chapter to an end.

Lord, make us instruments of thy peace;
Where hate rules, let us bring love,
Where malice, forgiveness,
Where disputes, reconciliation,
Where error, truth,
Where doubt, faith,
Where despair, hope,
Where darkness, Thy light,
Where sorrow, joy!
O Master, let us strive more to comfort others than to be comforted,
To understand others than to be understood,
To love others, more than to be loved!
For those who give, receive,
Those who forget, find,
And those who forgive, receive forgiveness,
And dying, we rise again to eternal life.[17]

Questions for Reflection and Discussion

- When we truly want what God wants, how does this desire affect our Christian life?
- How is temperament more important than technique in discernment?
- How did the interpretation of Romans 12:1 help you better understand discernment?

Chapter 9

WALKING WITH A
SERVANT'S HEART

I began this book with a story about my dad. Now I want to tell another one about him. I stated that he was a walker. Now I want to characterize him as a servant. Whether the activity had to do with the church, the community, the Boy Scouts, or the Little League, folks knew that all they had to do was "call Joe," and things would swing into action. For the most part, my dad resisted leadership positions, but everyone in town considered him a leader—a servant-leader. And from his quiet place behind the scenes, he likely got more done than if he had held public office.

My clear message is that praying to know God's will only makes sense against the backdrop of servanthood. Without this, it can become another ego-displaying enterprise. We can spiritualize praying for discernment when the truth is we're only posturing so folks will see us as poor, simple servants of Jesus. If we are not walking with a true servant's heart, we might as well abandon any posturing that makes us look like Christians who want to find and follow God's will. It's all for show. But the door swings open for those with a servant's heart because God knows we can be trusted to receive the revelation given to us by the Holy Spirit. We must continue to explore and develop the implications of what we have received. In this sense, discernment is a never-ending process. But it now occurs within the context of stewardship and trustworthiness. Servants can be trusted with the master's possessions.

I know of no better place to go in seeing what characterizes a servant than to John 13, where Jesus washes his disciples' feet. His words and deeds in this chapter exemplify walking with a servant's heart. His steps create a pathway for us to walk in becoming servants of God—men and women who will quietly, confidently, and effectively carry out God's will when they know it. So, let's follow in Jesus' footsteps and see what it means to walk with a servant's heart.

The first step comes in genuinely loving those around us. God is love. So God's will always reflects, communicates, and embodies love in some way. It may have to be "tough" love on occasion, but love always serves as the igniting motive in praying to know God's will. I have served in the church and community long enough to know the difference between loving service and other kinds. Some service is, as we have already noted, little more than self-aggrandizement. Some service is flat out manipulative. People with high control needs often gravitate to leadership positions, using their office as a platform for service, which under further investigation turns out to be impersonal and transactional, rather than truly relational.

Instead of this impersonal relationship, God calls us to be servants who live with compassion and authenticity. We have words that describe this living: "People care how much you know when they know how much you care." Living as servants brings manipulation to an end, putting in its place genuine love. Jesus' servanthood begins in love, which the Gospel of John describes, "Having loved his own who were in the world, he loved them to the end" (John 13:1). When Jesus left his seat at the table to wash the disciples' feet, he continued a pattern of service that he modeled from the beginning. Servanthood based upon genuine love appears natural rather than contrived or weighted down with secondary motives. It exudes a purity that people respond to. Perhaps the best testimony to servanthood is that people are sorry to see you go when it comes time to leave! Clearly Jesus' announced departure brought sadness to the disciples; they knew that from start to finish he had loved them.

When we pray to know God's will, we are really saying, "God, show me how to be a loving person in this situation." We may find God revealing to us what Martin Luther King Jr. called "strength to love" in the face of challenging circumstances. We may receive the call to embody compassionate love—the love that Jesus had as the good shepherd who loved and cared for the sheep—especially because they had no shepherd. We also may see patient love in Jesus who had to put up with so much messiness in his disciples. There's no end to what kind of love we may be asked to share in response to our praying to know God's will. But no matter the form, the core motive for praying at all is the desire for God's love to enter us and flow through us for the sake of others.

The second step in walking with a servant's heart is doing so against the backdrop of reality. The writer of John's Gospel does not soft-pedal what's going on: The devil had already put into Judas's heart the plan to betray Jesus. And Jesus knew it. Jesus' servanthood was not a "pie in the sky" action but rather a deed performed in the midst of his passion. He served in and through his pain. He laid aside more than his robe; he put down his own suffering (or at least moved it aside), so he could care for those who were with him—those who would shortly be turned every which way but loose as they experienced the fear and grief of his torture and death.

At times we pray to know God's will, but when it comes to us, our first response is, "Really?" The path leads through challenges we may never have thought we would face. Those who believe in a "prosperity gospel" cannot accept this path. They have to deny it or redefine it. Those around them who see what's going on have to reframe it, often concluding that their suffering friend must not have faith or this kind of thing would not be happening. But this is not the way of Jesus. Instead, he stared the darkest hours of his life in the face—and served anyway.

I will never forget the day one of my students knocked on my office door. David had stopped by to tell me his brain cancer had returned—and this time with an aggressiveness that was even more violent than his first bout. We cried, talked, and prayed. Barring a miracle, David would not live to graduate and begin the ministry he felt convinced that God had called him to. We prayed for him in class. We anointed him with oil in the seminary chapel. Folks all over the place (to say nothing of his family and friends) interceded for him. But . . . David died. We held his memorial service in the seminary chapel at the very hour he was supposed to be taking the final exam in my class. Through tear-filled eyes and with a broken voice, I was able to say to those of us who gathered to remember David that "he has passed with flying colors."

David and I had several long visits during his final days. Oh sure, David was deeply troubled. He could never make sense of his experience. He had one or two episodes in class, when we had to stop and care for him. His condition continued to worsen. But David was not alone. He knew the presence of the risen Christ, and that enabled him to stare death in the face. David remains one of the most courageous people I have ever known. To the end, David continued to serve God, his family, and the rest of us with all the energy he had. He did not slack one bit. His desire to be a good husband, father, student, and friend was as strong at the end as it had ever been. He prepared as thoroughly as if he had fifty years to minister in the church. David knew, lived, and witnessed to the fact that the only way to walk with a servant's heart is against the backdrop of reality.

The third step of walking with a servant's heart connects with what we have just noted. It is to be rooted in the confidence of a vital relationship with God. When we walk with a servant's heart what matters is *who* we walk with—not what we get out of the walking. This proves true especially when the road is rough and the way painful. But our service is filled with joy. Our service has accomplished its desired end. We have prayed to know God's will, have come to know it, and have carried it out. We have done what we were supposed to do. Our inquiry regarding God's will began in our confidence that God would lead us and guide us, and our execution of God's will moved forward with the same confidence. John says that Jesus knew he had come from God and was going to God (13:3); this bedrock foundation motivated his service from start to finish.

Something good happens in our souls when we discover that we find fulfillment in doing God's will by doing it. The responses of those around us, whether praise or blame, do not provide the meaning; God provides the meaning. When we pray, "Thy will be done," we affirm God's will as the primary goal; everything else is secondary. John Wesley conveyed this spirit to the early Methodists in the annual Covenant Renewal Service when they prayed that they would be God's servants whether full or empty, employed or unemployed, having all things or having nothing. We root our service in the confidence that we are God's beloved sons and daughters. Out of that conviction we go out to do the will of God on earth as it is in heaven.

We take **the fourth step** in walking with a servant's heart when we demonstrate our servanthood in actions, not merely words. A little later that same evening, Jesus told his disciples, "Love one another," and then added this phrase, "as I have loved you" (John 15:12). By the time he said these words, Jesus had already demonstrated the words through his deeds. His manner was his message, and his actions confirmed that what he said was not only true but could be lived out. Later the book of James would communicate the same message: "Faith by itself, if it has no works, is dead" (2:17). Jesus shows us that the title *servant* requires action.

One of my favorite *Peanuts* cartoons depicts Snoopy shivering in the cold. In the second frame, Charlie Brown and Linus observe Snoopy's plight. In the third frame, they tell Snoopy to "be of good cheer!" The final frame shows Snoopy sitting in the snow alone, still shivering. Nothing in Snoopy's situation changed because Charlie Brown and Linus took no action to make Snoopy warm. Servanthood is the same. We can preach and teach about it, sing about it, have conferences that emphasize it—but nothing happens until we do something.

Jesus was a servant not because he named himself one; he was a servant because he got up from the table, girded himself with a towel, and moved from one disciple to another washing their feet. The word *obedience* means listening with the intent of putting into practice what we hear. The only reason to pray to know God's will is our prior intention to put it into practice once we know it. "Love one another as I have loved you" turns a philosophy into a mission—an attitude into an action. And in the end, feet are clean and shivering people are warm. Most Christians and congregations do not flounder for lack of knowledge but for lack of doing something in Jesus' name.

A fifth step in walking with a servant's heart is persevering in the midst of resistance. Of all people, Peter tried to prevent Jesus from washing his feet. We cannot tell from the text whether Peter was the first person Jesus went to or whether he had washed a few others prior to arriving at Peter's feet. Regardless of the order, Jesus did not allow Peter's protest to cancel the ministry. Jesus' purpose defined his servanthood. Thankfully, Jesus' rebuke and honesty shook Peter into reality, and he allowed the Lord to wash his feet too. But I believe if Peter had kept his sandals on and put his feet under the table, Jesus would have moved on and kept going. He was not going to allow even his friend's resistance to prevent him from doing what God had sent him into the world to do.

Most people I know can tell of experiences where they had to forge ahead despite resistance. Pastors have been moved and workers have lost their jobs, but the retribution did not stop the truth from marching on. This is the witness of the martyrs. Over the centuries they could be killed, but the will of God could not be stopped. Servants know this. They do not have to win or even survive in order to live out God's desires for their lives. Walking with a servant's heart means not allowing resistance to cancel the program.

The final step that Jesus takes and reminds us to take is to use the moment to set subsequent ideas and actions in motion. He concluded the foot washing with these words, "I have set you an example" (John 13:15). What he had done they were now to do. True servanthood is not an end in itself; it is the commencement of a process. Servants model the will of God, so it can be done again. Jesus didn't end the foot washing with these words to call attention to himself but rather to be sure the disciples knew that he was giving them a pattern to follow in their own lives and ministries. As we read the rest of the New Testament, we see that his example "took," and they continued to do for others what Jesus had done for them.

As a pastor I always appreciated moving to a new church and finding ministry underway—ministry that previous pastors and laypersons had set in motion. The will of God does not have to be redone each time it needs to be done. Praying to know God's will is not a start-from-scratch enterprise. As we have noted, scripture and tradition reveal much of God's will. And much comes to us through the actions of men and women who have preceded us. Churches thrive on the basis of good examples. Walking with a servant's heart means doing some exemplification so that others realize their call to action. Walking with a servant's heart means exemplifying the will of God through concrete action. Our way of living out the will of God is not necessarily prescriptive of how others are called to do it, but our example illustrates that God's will must be carried out through specific actions.

Upon occasion, I wish I could go back in time and be present to learn firsthand from Jesus, being present to hear him teach and see him work. This evening with the disciples as recorded in John's Gospel is one of those times. Wouldn't it have been great to be in the room? But lacking that, we depend on the Gospel's account of what happened. To read this passage fully, we have to enter into it. This is holy drama. We have to feel it as well as think it. We have to put ourselves at the table and allow Jesus to wash our feet. For as surely as tomorrow comes after today, we will be called to do for others what Jesus has done for us. There is no way to pray to know the will of God apart from this. Discernment means walking with a servant's heart.

Questions for Reflection and Discussion

- What came to your mind when you read "the door [to discernment] swings open for those with a servant's heart "?
- Which step in walking with a servant's heart spoke most to you? Why?
- What is your response to the phrase "most Christians and congregations do not flounder for lack of knowledge but for lack of doing something in Jesus' name"?

Chapter 10

WALKING WITH A
BRILLIANT VIEW

All the world receives life-giving rays from the sun, but living in Florida affords me plenty of bright, sunshiny days. From the middle of October until the middle of April, most days burst with a brilliance that makes everything seem to stand out more than usual. I've had moments at the beach where the light was so illuminating it felt like I could see clear across the ocean. Jeannie and I have had wonderful times holding hands, walking silently—unable to take it all in. We have made precious memories while walking in the light.

As we come to the end of this book, I hope my suggestions will make your walk with God more meaningful and memorable. Perhaps the image of walking in the light has given you a metaphor for praying to know and do God's will. We have taken many steps in this journey. I want to close by stepping back and seeing the big picture of discernment, at least as I've tried to present it. Consider it like a homecoming from an enjoyable vacation and sharing your favorite photos with friends. It's impossible to capture it all, but you can select the moments that stand out the most.

The first photograph reminds us that praying to know God's will is not a technique. First and foremost, it is a disposition of your heart—a desire to be an agent through whom the two great commandments can be realized. The longer I have pondered discernment, the more it seems to be a disposition rather than a formula. The desire to know and do the will of God reflects an inclination of our hearts that God will honor. This desire does not result from saying and doing things in a particular way or according to a prescribed process. Knowing the will of God comes as blessing, an experience that arises after we have heard God say to us, "I love you," and we have responded, "I love you too." In the moment of heart-to-heart exchange, we gain impressions that form ideas. These ideas stay with us until we recognize they are meant to be turned into behaviors. Discernment is a way of life—the awakening that comes as we walk in the light of God.

I think this is why the mystics speak of their relationship with God either using the idea of marriage or a deep and abiding friendship with another person. They knew (and know) that when we experience the working of the Holy Spirit in our human spirit, something happens—something natural, unforced, and related to life as we actually live it. They often referred to this joint working as "ordinary holiness," and they considered nothing more wonderful than to share with God in a deep relationship of holy love. When we apply this to praying to know God's will, it means that insight flows from inclination. So, the most important question we can ask on the way to know and do the will of God is this: "Do I want to find and follow God more than anything else?"

We have this desire and ask this question because we are made in God's image. And this is **the second photograph** I want to show. Because we are made in the image of God, we can become cocreators with God, instruments in God's hands to craft life on this earth as God intends it. We are part of a never-ending revelation/response pattern—a pattern bigger than us and beyond us, but one that we periodically intersect as we walk through the days of our lives. God calls us to practice the presence of God so that the gaps between moments of awareness grow shorter and shorter. In this life we will never fully and finally close the gap, but we will find ourselves on a journey to that place where we will no longer see through a glass darkly but rather face to face. (See 1 Corinthians 13:12, KJV.) We find ourselves, as the context for that verse suggests, on a continued journey into the life of love—a journey that one day will be that of unbroken communion with the God who has made us, redeemed us, and sanctified us. In the meantime, all we can do is keep praying to know the will of God and celebrating (cherishing) those times when we know it and have the opportunity to do it. Such times offer keyhole glimpses into what will be a perpetual experience in eternity.

Turning to **a third photograph**, we see that being God's person in a situation is the aim of discernment—not taking a particular action in that situation. When we pray to know God's will, we pray to become a person in whom Christ dwells through the Spirit and through whom God works to manifest the fruit of the Spirit: love, joy, peace, patience, kindness, generosity, faithfulness, gentleness, and self-control. (See Galatians 5:22-23.) What that looks like in any given moment will be specific to the moment. But we pray to know God's will so that these qualities can define our experiences.

People remember these fruits long after they have forgotten the concrete behavior. So, as we pray to know God's will, we must say, "God, show me how to incarnate and express the fruit of the Spirit in my day, in my relationships, in my opportunities, in my challenges."

This approach requires that we become learners all our days. That's why I included chapters on learning to pray to know God's will through the insights of scripture and tradition. Here are **two additional photographs** to keep in our journey scrapbook. The Bible is the book of God, and tradition is the book of the church. Together they chronicle at least six thousand years of lived theology— sixty centuries of human experience. How could any of us presume to know how to pray to know God's will apart from the insights that these inspirational records have left us? If we sincerely want to be people of discernment, we will be people of the Book and people of the church. We will run our race, soaking up the inspiration of the great cloud of witnesses and looking to Jesus, the author and finisher of our faith. (See Hebrews 12:1-2, KJV.)

We do all of this in community—**another essential photograph** in our discernment album. The whole remains greater than the sum of its parts. Interaction with others enlarges and expands our ideas and impressions. Holy conversation enriches our ability to know and do God's will. Comments from others can keep us from making mistakes we would later regret. They can put the flesh of action on the bones of insight, so that what we want to do is what we actually end up doing. The community both protects and promotes. Discernment may begin with an individual insight or impression but usually it matures and deepens in community.

This brings us to **the final photograph** in the album that leaves us with the big picture. We learn that despite our devotion and desire to find and follow God's will, we will not always get it right. We fail, falter, and fall short. Discernment is less about correctness than about consecration. Yet, if initial attentiveness initiates the discernment process, ongoing attentiveness keeps it moving—not always in a straight line but forward in the sense of pleasing God by the sincerity of attitude and action.

We learn as much from our mistakes as from our successes. We grow from our setbacks as well as from our advances. Both experiences come as blessings because God teaches us in and through all things. All is grace. Our consolations and our desolations are means by which God guides us. The primary fear in praying to know God's will is that we allow our perfectionism to keep us from pursuing any action.

As we close the album on our journey to find and follow God's will, we do so with the spirit of humility. We know that discernment is of God, not of works—lest any of us should boast. We respond to and follow the God who leads. In this spirit we move forward with a sense of adventure and joy in our praying to know God's will.

Questions for Reflection and Discussion

- Which of the "photographs" helped you most? Why?
- How has your reading of this book enriched your knowledge and practice of discernment?
- Now that you have completed this book, what do you think God would have you do next to keep your journey of discernment moving forward?

NOTES

1. The Bible bears witness to this from Genesis to Revelation. Paul specifically refers to it in Romans 12:2.

2. The Bible bears witness to this in general through its use of words such as *love, mercy,* and *grace.* John specifically declares it in 1 John 4:16.

3. J. Ellsworth Kalas, *The Will of God in an Unwilling World* (Louisville, KY: Westminster John Knox, 2011), 61.

4. The *false self* is a term that describes the egocentric life. It is the life that humanity has lived after the Fall in Genesis 3. For more on this subject, see M. Robert Mulholland Jr.'s *The Deeper Journey: The Spirituality of Discovering Your True Self* (Downer's Grove, IL: InterVarsity Press, 2006); Richard Rohr's *Falling Upward: A Spirituality for the Two Halves of Life* (San Francisco: Jossey-Bass, 2013); and Joyce Rupp's *Open the Door: A Journey to the True Self* (Notre Dame, IN: Ave Maria Press, 2008).

5. Confirmation is part of the larger ministry of Christian education. In early Christianity confirmation began with catechesis—the purpose of which was to lead persons to a profession of faith and baptism (or a remembrance of their baptism). But even after that, the formative process continued with teaching (*didache*).

6. The earliest use of the phrase "take and read" occurs in Saint Augustine's *Confessions.* After that, it can be found in a host of writings across the centuries, including a contemporary book by Eugene Peterson titled *Take and Read: Spiritual Reading* (Grand Rapids, MI: Eerdmans, 1996).

7. The idea of "savoring" a passage came to me through the counsel Baron Von Hugel gave to Evelyn Underhill; the

image of a passage as a lozenge that's allowed to dissolve slowly on our tongues.

8. Interestingly and importantly, this rising awareness has changed my experience of corporate worship. It does not have to be "inspirational," "good," or in my preferred style. I enter into worship with a *lectio*-expectancy, that even a morsel of God's word is a meal. And in every time and form of worship, that kind of spiritual food is present.

9. M. Robert Mulholland, *Shaped by the Word: The Power of Scripture in Spiritual Formation* (Nashville, TN: Upper Room Books, 2001).

10. The phrase "strangely warmed" is one John Wesley used to describe the condition of his heart on May 24, 1738, during his experience with God in the small-group meeting on Aldersgate Street in London. The journal entry that he wrote is found in Volume 18 of *The Works of John Wesley*, Bi-Centennial Edition, edited by Reginald Ward and Richard Heitzenrater (Nashville, TN: Abingdon Press, 1988), 250.

11. Happily, these conferences are in the public domain and accessible via the Christian Classics Ethereal Library (www.ccel.org). An acceptable history of Cassian can also be found via Wikipedia. For a more in-depth study, I recommend the volume on John Cassian published by Paulist Press as part of their multivolume series The Classics of Western Spirituality. And Owen Chadwick's *John Cassian* (Cambridge: Cambridge University Press, 1968), is arguably still the best study of Cassian and early Christian monasticism.

12. Terrence G. Kardong, *Benedict's Rule: A Translation and Commentary* (Collegeville, MN: Liturgical Press, 1996), 34.

13. I do not mean that the use of Robert's Rules of Order is always inappropriate. I am speaking of praying to know

God's will, and I have come to believe that a consensus approach is preferable in times of discernment. I personally believe that consensus can also work in church business matters, but I respect the use of the more formal process when an actual vote is needed.

14. This is not an otherworldly concept because in the Incarnation the Word became flesh. In fact, it is Christlikeness that keeps Christian spirituality truly human; that is, where the tangible and the intangible come together into a real life. Without this, we can distort spirituality into something that can be professed without actually being lived.

15. Brother Lawrence, *The Practice of the Presence of God* (New York: Fleming Revell, n.d). Brother Lawrence uses different phrases to describe this experience, but it has come to be called "the prayer of referral." That is, when we become aware of any distraction from our gaze upon God, we simply refer that awareness to God and then not bother ourselves any further with dwelling upon it. It may be a simple mistake or a grievous sin; whatever it is, we ask for God to take it, revive us, and move on.

16. Paul actually uses several main Greek words that are translated "mind" in English. But they all share the quality of wholehearted perceptiveness—that is, a way of "thinking" that engages the entire person—a way of "thinking" that brings our wills into conformity with our discoveries. John Wesley called this characteristic "living faith."

17. This prayer exists in multiple versions in the public domain. I have chosen to use a version of it that I carry in my Bible. The original source for this particular translation is unknown, as is the date of its composition.

FOR FURTHER READING

The following reading list is intentionally brief. It allows you to continue the journey you have begun with this book, expanding on some of its themes.

Discernment

Bieber, Nancy. *Decision Making and Spiritual Discernment: The Sacred Art of Finding Your Way.* Woodstock, VT: Skylight Paths, 2010.

Doughty, Stephen and Melissa Tidwell. *The Way of Discernment.* Nashville, TN: Upper Room Books, 2008. Companions in Christ series.

Job, Rueben P. *A Guide to Spiritual Discernment.* Nashville, TN: Upper Room Books, 1996.

Johnson, Ben Campbell. *Discerning God's Will.* Louisville, KY: Westminster/John Knox Press, 1990.

Morris, Danny and Charles Olsen. *Discerning God's Will Together: A Spiritual Practice for the Church.* Nashville, TN: Upper Room Books, 1997.

Muto, Susan and Adrian Van Kaam. *Divine Guidance: Seeking to Find and Follow the Will of God.* Ann Arbor, MI: Servant Publications, 1994.

Lectio Divina

Benner, David G. *Opening to God: Lectio Divina and Life as Prayer.* Downers Grove, IL: InterVarsity Press, 2010.

Casey, Michael. *Sacred Reading: The Ancient Art of Lectio Divina.* Liguori, MO: Liguori Publications, 1996.

Mulholland, Robert. *Shaped by the Word: The Power of Scripture in Spiritual Formation.* Nashville, TN: Upper Room Books, 2000.

Thompson, Marjorie. *The Way of Scripture.* Nashville, TN: Upper Room Books, 2010.

Befriending the Saints

Dunnam, Maxie. *The Workbook on Keeping Company with the Saints.* Nashville, TN: Upper Room Books, 2001.

Foster, Richard. *Streams of Living Water: Celebrating the Great Traditions of the Christian Faith.* San Francisco: Harper Collins, 2010.

Hansen, Gary. *Kneeling with Giants: Learning to Pray with History's Best Teachers.* Downers Grove, IL: InterVarsity Press, 2012.

A Surrendered Life

De Caussade, Jean-Pierre. *Abandonment to Divine Providence.* A devotional classic available in many different editions.

Jones, E. Stanley. *Victory through Surrender: Self-Realization through Self-Surrender.* Nashville, TN: Abingdon Press, 1980.

Lawrence, Brother. *The Practice of the Presence of God.* A devotional classic available in many different editions.

ABOUT THE AUTHOR

DR. STEVE HARPER (PhD, Duke University, 1981) is a retired elder in the Florida Annual Conference of The United Methodist Church and also a retired professor who taught in the disciplines of spiritual formation and Wesley studies. He has been married to Jeannie for forty-four years, and they have two children and three grandchildren.

Steve has authored sixteen books and coauthored thirteen others, as well as numerous articles and entries for Christian encyclopedias. He has also worked on several Bible projects, including The Upper Room Spiritual Formation Bible.

In retirement, Steve and Jeannie are enjoying a more contemplative life, including travels all around the country in Jeannie's "Little Red Truck" with their pop-up camper.